Study Tips

How to Study Effectively and Get Better Grades

By William H. Armstrong

Winner of the
National School Bell Award
for distinguished interpretation in the
field of education and author of the
Newbery Medal award-winning
book, "Sounder."

Kent School

Kent, Connecticut

Barron's Educational Series, Inc., Woodbury, New York

All inquiries should be addressed to:

Barron's Educational Series, Inc.
113 Crossways Park Drive
Woodbury, New York 11797

International Standard Book No. 0-8120-0608-9

Library of Congress Catalog Card No. 75-16482

Library of Congress Cataloging in Publication Data
Armstrong, William Howard, 1914_
A Handbook of Study Tips
A Handbook of Study Tips
1. Study, Method of. I. Title.

LB1049.A69 371.3'02812 75-16482

ISBN 0-8120-0608-9 pbk.

PRINTED IN THE UNITED STATES OF AMERICA

Contents

CHAPTER 1

The Gifts With Which You Work

CHAPTER 2

Listening: The Easy Way to Learn

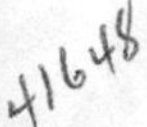

CHAPTER 3

The Classroom: Atmosphere for Achievement

CHAPTER 4

Study Time: Design for Success

CHAPTER 5

Mastering Assignments: Methods of Study

CHAPTER 6

Summaries and Outlines: Using Them and Learning from Them

CHAPTER 7

Words: How to Improve Your Knowledge of Them

CHAPTER 8

Words: Making Them Work for You

CHAPTER 9

Spelling and Punctuation: Hallmarks of Completion

CHAPTER 10

Books: The Memory of Mankind

CHAPTER 11

Reading: Faster with More Understanding

CHAPTER 12

The Library: How to Use It

CHAPTER 13

Written Work: The Product and Its Package

CHAPTER 14

Written Work: Research Themes, Book Reports, and Style

CHAPTER 15

Tests and Examinations: The Big Score

CHAPTER 16

Motivation: Each Must Find It for Himself

CHAPTER 1

The Gifts With Which You Work

Introduction: From these roots

You will never find the mythical treasure at the end of the rainbow, but you have been endowed with a treasury of gifts far more precious than dreams of gold at the feet of many rainbows. In this chapter a baker's dozen of your wonderful gifts, and how they are ever available to help you grow, will be mentioned. These are not all of your gifts, and out of these many others grow. Unless you neglect them, ignore them, distort them, and destroy them finally with fear and false values, they will provide the raw material from which you will grow into the person you wish to be—improving your marks in school and finding the happy life by doing what you can with what you have To point that way for you is the aim of this book.

So much has been said and written about the necessity for good grades that it sometimes seems that the most important element in preparing for your future is overlooked. It is important to get good grades, for never has the competition for available places in the world of work been so great. Neither has the future of those who fail ever been so limited. But let us not lose sight of that important word—growth.

It is the purpose of this book to provide you with simple and sincere suggestions for using the unique gifts which were given you, not only to improve your grades, but to indicate to you that training in algebra, history, and French is incomplete without that peculiar growth of spirit, feeling, and desire which gives learning its total meaning. The aim is not only to help you achieve the excellent marks you need to enter college, but to have you enter college with a full knowledge of the wonderful gifts you were given. With a mature sense of responsibility and obligation, you can best use these gifts to satisfy your own self-respect and the dream potentials of those who, in small ways and great, contribute to your opportunities.

The gift of individuality

The *first* of the wonderful gifts provided you is that of individuality. This might seem paradoxical at first reflection because you have probably experienced the frustration of wondering how you can become an individual. Let this disturb you no longer. Your rebellion against the pressure of parents, teachers, and environment to make you like others sometimes leads you to extremes in trying to be different. Although this is part of your growth toward maturity and adulthood, it should consume very little of your precious time and energy, for there is no one else in the whole world like you. Neither can a pattern for physical or spiritual growth be fitted to any two people. Your growth will be along lines as distinctly unique as your own individuality. However, you can be helped by the application of experiences which have been useful to others. You can direct your development along paths that will bring the most satisfaction to you and to those around you.

The gift of self-confidence

The second of your natural gifts, sometimes lying so still within you—waiting to be used—that you convince yourself that you do not have it, is self-confidence. It can, like most of our gifts of life, atrophy and become useless. It is therefore important, no matter how inadequate you have felt, to be aware of its presence within you and to build it into a strong fortress of self-assurance.

Somehow it seems that adult leadership tends toward blame rather than praise. A feeling of inferiority slows and smothers self-assurance and you are sometimes forced to bolster your confidence by a false "front"—pretending indifference. Even though the pretense may be accompanied by noisy braggadocio, you really feel terribly inadequate and unhappy with life. If you can be made aware of your assets, capabilities, and strong points, you will no longer resent having your weaknesses pointed out by your elders. For we all have weaknesses—young and old alike. Once you know your weaknesses, you can direct particular aids to growth toward making weaknesses into strengths. Therefore, if a teacher tells you that you have difficulty listening in class, that your handwriting is poor, or that your test papers show extreme nervousness, do not accept these as permanent weaknesses. Let your wonderful innate gift of self-confidence move within you. It is there—ready to make strengths out of weaknesses with only a little patient help from you. Do not be discouraged. The most important and fundamental changes that result from growing into a self-assured individual do not take place in days or weeks or months. The practices and suggestions that you accept to help you write better themes will grow in effectiveness to insure your writing better business letters, contracts, news-stories, or whatever you will find yourself writing after your formal education is finished. Self-confidence, if allowed to work for you through constructive and tried experiences and habits, grows to meet the demands of added responsibilities which life offers as a challenge to those who are capable. Don't say, "I can't write a good algebra test because I am careless." Say, "My algebra tests this year are an improvement over what I did last year." Make it so by exerting constructive effort to improve, and by having confidence in your ability to improve.

The gift of desire

The third of your natural gifts is the desire to enhance and improve, and to improve is to learn. Some people are extremely lucky to have a parent or teacher who so stimulates this desire that it becomes a tireless drive to improve and an insatiable hunger to learn. Abraham Lincoln's mother read the Bible by the light of an open fire in a wilderness cabin. Though she died when the boy was only nine, she left him with a burning desire to coax beauty from language. He fed this hunger on a few great works of literature. His ability to say what men felt in their hearts but could not utter was perhaps the primary factor in making Lincoln one of history's immortals rather than an unknown backwoods lawyer.

Ben Franklin's desire for self-improvement would not let the self-made editor and printer retire at forty-five, although he had both fame and fortune. He went on to become a scientist, inventor, governor, public servant, diplomat, and one of the world's most beloved men. The pages of the lives of the great afford innumerable examples. The desire for improvement gave an Italian boy named Angelo Roncalli the strength and endurance he needed to walk three miles daily over the mountain from Sotto il Monte to Calano to attend school. He became Pope John XXIII.

Your desire now is to improve your grades and succeed in school. Be sure that this wonderful gift is never replaced by mundane wanting. Luxury, gadgetry, and creature comforts are false symbols of civilization—the pagan idols of our times. Desire for yourself the right to grow and live a significant life—to train your intellect, develop your character, and acquire the ability to solve the new problems which shall confront you by applying the accumulated wisdom provided by your education.

The gift of will

The gift of will, the power to put life into dreams, follows desire in natural sequence. Desire dwindles to a faltering, shadowy, half forgotten dream unless it is willed into reality. Feeling, thinking, and willing are often designated as the three basic functions of the mind. Something is felt to be worthwhile, good to do or have; it is thought about, evaluated, measured mentally for advantage or importance; but unless the mind wills to accomplish it there remains only a dream or an intention unfulfilled. The people who have accomplished the most in the world are those who were dreamers first and then willed to make their dreams come true.

Louis Pasteur is an example of one of the world's best students. He willed to learn and made his dreams of alleviating the problems and suffering of his fellow men a reality. If possible you should read a biography of this remarkable man. If his work had not resulted in saving unnumbered millions of lives, the inspiration of his life and the direction he set for himself would have ensured him a place among the world's great men. While still a young student he pasted on his desk the three words that would direct his life—"Will, Work, Wait." At the age of nineteen he was a science teacher. In a letter to his sisters he wrote, "To will is a great thing, for Action and Work follow Will, and almost always Work is accompanied by Success. Will opens doors; Works passes them; and Success is waiting to crown one's efforts." When Pasteur's life ended fifty-four years later, the whole world had come to know and appreciate what the nineteen-year-old science teacher had written his sisters.

From the gift of will comes valuable by-products: ambition, determination, persistence, and patience. Will, like all your other wonderful gifts, must become more than accepted ingredients of your life or passive beliefs. Will must be used. It must become habit, just as being an individual, having self-confidence, desiring improvement, and all other endowments must be used and become habit. It was William James, the psychologist and philosopher, who said, "Could the young but realize how soon they will become mere walking bundles of habits, they would give more heed to their conduct while in the plastic state. We are spinning our own fates, good or evil, and never to be undone."

The gift of conscience

Many of the natural gifts which are given you become inactive unless they are used and nourished. Conscience is the most indestructible, constant, and hard-working of all your spiritual tools. Determining what is right is not confined to the young; it is a problem that exists as long as life itself. What is right and what is wrong changes from age to age and from one society to another. Almost every decision that calls for you to make a judgment of right or wrong is different from any decision previously made. As you build character by application of your natural gifts and external influences, so you also develop standards; and your conscience is constantly checking against changes. Growth in ideas of right and wrong goes along with growth of the individual. When you find yourself doing something which you formerly thought was wrong, you say aloud to yourself, "Is this not still wrong or have I changed?" Sometimes it might be puzzling, and you might wonder whether your standards are "growing up or down." You will only wonder through a short period of growing pains, for if you listen to your conscience you will know that which is right even though a thousand voices raise a loud chorus to the contrary. It is your conscience, a constant and hard-working companion, that helps you through the tangled web of conflicting desires, inclinations, and advice from many sources, to a set of standards, grown from your own personal convictions. When you have worked your way through this tangle you have arrived at maturity. Once you have arrived at maturity your conscience begins immediately to help you toward a "philosophy of life." You may not always be completely happy with the gift of conscience, particularly when it speaks quiet disapproval against the behavior of the crowd you are with. Just remember that it is always working for you.

"But what," you ask, "has all this to do with how I can improve my grades?"

"All this," we reply, "has a great part in how you can improve your grades."

In the beginning it was stated that both training and growth give learning its total meaning. You will, before you finish this book, understand the significance of your God-given gifts and the part they must play in whatever you do that makes you more than what you were—whether it be better grades or increased respect for yourself and those around you. But neither education nor better grades are accomplishments that appear suddenly. So before we begin to answer your question (and impatience is at your age an important temporary gift) let's look at some more of the glorious attributes sustained, nurtured, and passed on to you as a part of your legacy from the human family to which you belong. Dr. Albert Einstein had some thoughts aligned to the individual and the meaning of growth:

The individual, if left alone from birth, would remain primitive and beast-like in his thoughts and feelings to a degree that we can hardly conceive. The individual is what he is and has the significance that he has not so much in virtue of his individuality, but rather as a member of a great human society, which directs his material and spiritual existence from the cradle to the grave.[1]

The gift of perception

Perception is the endowment which played an important part in giving the designation "homo sapiens" (wise man) to your ancestors and separated them from the other animals. Perception is the first method of learning; it is the first primary reason for education; it is the gift, serving mind and senses, whereby you become acquainted with the world around you, your place in that world, and the world which is within you.

Perception, and the two gifts that follow it in order —thought and communication—constitute a major part

[1]Albert Einstein, *The World As I See It* (New York: The Philosophical Library, 1949).

of the dynamics of growth and achievement for the individual. By perception you take in all that nourishes and provides growth for your mental and spiritual growth, just as you take in food for your physical development. The eagle or hawk, soaring high over a valley, has also been endowed with a gift of perception. But the nature of the gift is different; it is for survival—a search for food and an awareness of danger. Our gift of perception surpasses survival; it is the ability to see that which is possible.

Perception is the ability that makes meaningful experiences possible. From meaningful experiences come changes in attitudes and habits. Certain attitudes and habits are sometimes very strongly established, but none are strong enough to withstand a keen perceptive power that can visualize the fuller meaning or the better way. The power of perception must go beyond mere awareness of one's surroundings. It must perceive purpose and the action this purpose dictates.

History offers many illustrations of men who used their perceptive powers to achieve success. The story of Joseph in the Book of Genesis, which Leo Tolstoi called the perfect short story, is also one of the world's greatest success stories. Joseph was a slave and prisoner in the stone quarries, an alien—completely alone in a strange land and numbered among the dead by his kinsmen. His chance audience with the pharaoh came because Joseph had a reputation as a dreamer and an interpreter of dreams. But Joseph was more than a dreamer. Had it not been for keen perception, Joseph might well have been taken back to the stone quarries after he had told the pharaoh that his dream meant that there would be seven years of plenty followed by seven years of famine. But Joseph gave purpose to what he had perceived which resulted in experience and power that insured him forever against returning to the quarries. He suggested to the pharaoh that granaries and storehouses be built and filled with surplus grain during the seven years of plenty to feed the people when famine came to the land. You know the end of the story. Pharaoh made Joseph the vice-pharaoh and put him in charge of the whole program of preparation for the years of famine. Joseph saw with his eyes and his mind and acted upon the purpose he had visualized. This is keen perception—perception that sees through to the end.

Augustus Caesar was one of the world's most successful rulers. He literally ruled the known world from 31 B.C. to 14 A.D., yet in stature, demeanor, and appearance he seemed almost insignificant when compared to his famous uncle Julius or to mighty and forceful men such as Trajan and Diocletian. Always in ill health, he was endowed with an almost uncanny ability to perceive that which was possible in the vast Roman world. This seems to have been the gift which not only balanced the scales for him between success and failure, but made him almost totally successful.

There is a wonderful story of a boy who arrived at a newspaper office in response to a help wanted advertisement. Much to his dismay there were twenty-three boys ahead of him in the line. A keen sense of perception solved the problem which had momentarily confronted him. He wrote on the back of an envelope: "Dear Sir, I am twenty-third in line. Please do not hire anyone until you have talked to me." He then folded the envelope and asked the person in front of him to pass it forward to the person doing the interviewing. The interviewer read the note and continued to speak with each applicant, but the sharp perceptive sense of the boy twenty-third in line got him the job.

An amusing and true story may perhaps alert you to a state of constant watchfulness for putting this precious gift to work. A French teacher, five days before examination time, filled the blackboard in his classroom with material—verbs, sentences in English, sentences in French, lists of words, etc. He taught a total of sixty students, and daily they sat in his classroom for five days. When the examination was passed out there was a loud chorus of groans. Where had they seen this before—it had been on the blackboard for five days. Two people out of sixty had used their keen perceptive powers. They made perfect scores; the other fifty-eight made generally what the teacher expected—the level of achievement that they had made during the term. Perception is the gift which acquaints you with the world around you. It is a precious gift. Use it fully, constantly, and wisely. Be sure you are seeing when you look.

The gift of thought

Perception without thought brings neither conscious purpose nor action. So the gift of thought, that ability which designates man as the thinking animal, is the one without which all your other gifts would lie dormant or wither away to nothingness, leaving only the basic animal instincts. Thought is that most excellent of endowments which enables you to choose from your myriad perceptions that which can best benefit your life. Your whole education is designed to bring growth to your ability to think. If this were not so the number of thought puzzles which increase with each year of your life would overwhelm you. And life is indeed made up of thought puzzles upon which you must act daily.

The gift of thought provides the human mind with the capacity to deal in abstractions. A sound, for example, is an abstraction which can be converted into deep feeling. It can also be made into a symbol—a spoken word. Man has the further ability to record (write) the spoken word and make it into something visible and concrete. The gift of thought has made man "homo faber" (man the maker) as well as "homo sapiens." From this gift come all the valuable things that make our world: material things ranging all the way from the first flint-hatchet of the cave man to the most advanced, earth-circling rocket; and immaterial things—religion and morals, institutions such as home and community, also qualities and standards.

Let us quote again from Dr. Albert Einstein's beautiful book, *The World as I See It*:

Only the individual can think, and thereby create new values for society —nay, even set up new moral standards to which the life of the community conforms. Without creative, independently thinking and judging personalities the upward develop-

ment of society is as unthinkable as the development of the individual personality without the nourishing soil of the community.

The gift of communication

Communication and community come from the same root word, and without the ability to communicate the community would not be possible. Through the gift of communication you will receive your education, and the extent to which you develop the ability to communicate with others will help determine the success or failure of your life. The memory of mankind—its total knowledge and beliefs—is communicated to you through the medium of language. This gift of communication, it has been suggested, is the principal factor in raising us above the beasts and giving us dominion over them. "The individual, if left alone from birth, would remain primitive and beastlike in his thoughts and feelings to a degree that we can hardly conceive."

The gift of communication not only makes possible your receiving the legacy of wisdom from the ages, but makes you the guardian of it for those who come after you. "Bear in mind," said one of the wisest of men in speaking to a group of school children, "that the wonderful things you learn in your schools are the work of many generations, produced by enthusiastic effort and infinite labour in every country of the world. All this is put into your hands as your inheritance in order that you may receive it, honour it, add to it, and one day faithfully hand it on to your children. Thus do we mortals achieve immortality in the permanent things which we create in common."

From the time you first communicated with the world around you until the time you perhaps stand and put into words the deep feelings of men less able to communicate their ideas, you have daily increased the capacity of this wonderful gift; and this ability can be improved every day that we live. We hear that Winston Churchill was one of the world's great masters at the art of communication, that it was this ability which stirred the British first, and then the world, into action against Hitler. An American correspondent cabled in one story to America: "Winston Churchill has mobilized the English language and sent it into battle." Indeed, he had done just that—and he won. When he became prime minister in England's "darkest hour" he communicated to his people what they knew but feared to utter: "I have nothing to offer but blood and toil, tears and sweat." When Belgium had surrendered, France fallen, and the German army stood on the French coast and stared menacingly across at the white cliffs of Dover, Churchill communicated to his countrymen the defiant and resolute feeling which needed to be given voice:

We shall defend our island, whatever the cost may be. We shall fight on the beaches. We shall fight on the landing grounds. We shall fight on

the fields and in the streets. We shall fight in the hills. We shall never surrender. Let us brace ourselves to our duties, and so bear ourselves that, if the British Empire and Commonwealth last for a thousand years, men will say: This was their finest hour.

It is well within the confines of reason to say that this one man, who from the time he first fell in love with the English sentence as a boy in school—and incidentally that was about all he liked about formal education during most of his school years—with this outstanding gift, which he constantly worked to improve, did more than any other single man to win World War II. But this master of the gift of communication never ceased his efforts to improve. An assistant secretary of the navy rode a night train from Washington to Ottawa, Canada, on December 29, 1941, with Churchill, who was to address the Canadian Parliament the following day. From the secretary comes the story that the Prime Minister worked all night over the closing sentences of his speech. Here is one of them: "The invaders and tyrants must be made to feel that their fleeting triumphs will have a terrible reckoning, and that they are hunted men and that their cause is doomed." After the war Churchill was awarded the Nobel Prize in literature, not only for his writing but his wartime speeches against "a monstrous tyranny never surpassed in the dark, lamentable catalog of human crimes."

The world may never require of you such exertion of your gift of communication, but you must never cease working to increase the power of this great gift. In high school and college the degree of success you attain in communicating what you have learned to your teachers will constitute their sole means of grading your work—both oral and written. Communication is also achieved and supplemented by means other than words—pictures, a wave of the hand, a glance, a touch. To the sick child a father's hand on its forehead probably carries a greater message than a hundred words. And who has not found the meaning of a whole book in the tender grasp of a single hand. However, words constitute your principal medium for using this gift in your learning and in your life. Too much could never be said about the gift of communication. If you think too much has been quoted from one of the great masters of this gift, it will possibly surprise you to learn that you have something in common with him. Winston Churchill was probably speaking what you feel when he said, "Personally I am always ready to learn, although I do not always like being taught." If you are "ready to learn" it is all right for you not to have any great love for "being taught." Your better self, using your manifold gifts, will take care of your problems.

Perception, thought, and communication – these make masters over the other animals—these make possible the memory of the past—these provide the vision and dream of the future—these are the chief ingredients of learning—these are the basic reasons for education.

The gift of memory

Through your gift of memory you are the inheritor of knowledge, protecting laws, edifying arts, labor-saving and comfort-producing skills, and ideas and ideals of countless enduring things which make your life far more meaningful than that lived by your remote ancestors. They had little to reflect back upon and so they lived in fear of nature's unrelenting laws and their own capricious gods, following unquestionable taboos and totems. Memory provides you with a foundation upon which to erect your house of life. From the storehouse of memory you draw previous experiences—experiences that failed or proved durable to those who tried them. You select wisely and build your own experiences upon foundation stones tested by those who came before you.

In 1949 the British writer, George Orwell, published a terrifying book entitled *Nineteen Eighty-Four.* The story relates how a new political party, the Party of the Big Brother, takes over the whole of human society by enslaving men's minds. This is accomplished by destroying men's memory. First the memory of history is erased. After this the party can introduce its slogans: "War is Peace—Slavery is Freedom—Ignorance is Strength." Robbed of the memory of language, speech, and reason, man is set chartless and without direction in a world where past experience has become meaningless. He is taught that hate is a virtue and that memory, even the fleeting memory of a loved one, is the greatest of all crimes.

The gift of memory is so much a part of you that you take it for granted. Only by seeing what kind of animalistic existence you would endure without it, only when you are shown, as in *Nineteen Eighty-Four*, that save for the gift of memory you could have the very sound of your voice changed into the quacking of a duck, only then does memory suddenly stand out in its unique preciousness.

The gift of imagination

Memory maps for us the well-traveled roads of custom and tradition, as well as the exciting, little-used trails of those who at the crossroads of the known put into use the gift of imagination and find new adventure, new trails, new worlds. Imagination is the gift you can use to excite your English teacher with a story that is different, your history teacher with a new point of view, and your mathematics teacher with a new approach to the solution of a problem.

Imagination is that gift within you that sends you trailing intuition with the persistence of a foxhound after a hot scent, and sends you in pursuit of inspiration with the speed of an eagle answering the cry of her young when an enemy has found her nest. Inspiration, like the helpless young, is easily lost; falling down the crags of doubt and indifference into the abyss of procrastination. Given wings of imagination, it soars to heights of achievement.

There is of course a similarity between the gift of perception and that of imagination. Imagination is certainly, to a degree at least, perception "souped-up" with dual carburetors. Joseph Conrad, a Polish seaman who did not learn English until after he was twenty, but became one of Britain's greatest stylists and novelists—writing nothing until after he was forty—said this of imagination: "Only in men's imagination does every truth find an effective and undeniable existence. Imagination, not invention, is the supreme master of art as of life." This was written when Conrad was fifty-five, in a book entitled *A Personal Record*. He had, during the fifteen years between the age of forty and fifty-five, published half a dozen great sea novels. Surely he had used his gift of imagination fully. It is significant that he used the phrase "every truth" rather than "every dream," for whatever dreams his imagination had conjured up as he stood the long night watches on the dark and lonely sea had now become true.

Robert Louis Stevenson, the frail genius who lived much of his life in places of lonely banishment, used the gift of imagination to find beauty in ugliness. In an essay entitled *On the Enjoyment of Unpleasant Places* he wrote: "Things looked at patiently from one side after another generally end by showing a side that is beautiful." The gift of imagination provides vision beyond the negative and destructive forces of nature and the selfishness, greed, and injustice of the world, where according to the poet, James Russell Lowell, there is: "Truth forever on the scaffold, wrong forever on the throne." Only the gift of imagination gives vision to the experience of mystery—that profound reason and radiant beauty whose presence was a certainty to the poet: "But that scaffold sways the future, and behind the dim unknown standeth God within the shadow, keeping watch above his own." "The ingredients of imagination are," says Montaigne, one of the world's greatest essayists, "vision, sympathy, and sincerity." And he added, "I gather the flowers by the wayside, by the brooks and in the meadows, and only the string with which I bind them together is my own."

Test your own gift of imagination on the old Austrian folktale which follows:

Three young wayfarers stopped at noon to rest beneath a great oak tree. All three were butcher's apprentices. One looked at the oak tree and said, "What fine fat pigs could be grown from the acorns which fall from this oak." The second looked and said, "What a great supply of bark with which to tan our pig skins." The third looked and exclaimed, "What a fine mast this oak would make for a white-sailed ship to sail far-away oceans."

John Masefield ran away from home to become a sailor at the age of fifteen and spent part of his life sorting yarn in a rug factory in Yonkers, New York. When he was fifty he was made poet laureate of England. In his poem "Sea-Fever" he wrote: ". . . all I ask is a tall ship and a star to steer her by." Use your gift of imagination to help you believe in your star and steer your course by it.

The gift of time

Time is the gift given you to devote to the development and growth of all your other gifts. Time is a limited and sometimes frustrating gift. If used properly you count it a blessing; if squandered or allowed to dribble away, a glance backward at the futility of trying to retrieve it makes it one of life's starkest tragedies. However, time well spent might seem to show little or no growth; this too can be frustrating. It should not be. If you use your time wisely, you can wait in confidence that you will come to an awareness of the fruits thereof. This too, though you grow impatient not seeing immediate results, is time wisely spent. No one has ever equated a small beginning with a waste of time. When nature wishes to grow a tall and beautiful hemlock to stand against a winter sky and beautify the world, she takes a hundred years, but she grows a head of lettuce in six weeks.

Two enemies are always lurking near to rob you of the gift of time. One is procrastination and the other is disorder. Through lack of organization you adapt yourself to habits that lead you into time-wasting practices; and common human failing gives you an excuse foı delay. The materials of efficiently educating yourself and being successful in life are economy of energy and economy of time. Your education will remain tragically incomplete until you have learned to do the things you have to do when you ought to do them.

If your education is significantly complete you will have learned to use the little bits of time that add up to achievement. In 1901 a twenty-two-year-old mathematics graduate of the University of Zurich took a job in the Patent Office in Berne, Switzerland. He found that the job afforded many little bits of free time between the duties assigned to him. Instead of using this time to make paperclip chains, gossip with other office personnel, and institute the "coffee break" (it had to wait for someone else) he worked out the first theory of relativity. The young Patent Office employee's name was Albert Einstein. In the wilderness of Indiana, Dennis Hanks, Levi Hall, and several other young frontiersmen chopped wood and cleared land together. When they took "a breather" to "catch their wind" one of them would open a book and read as he sat on a stump. The rest thought him "peculiar." The peculiar backwoodsman who had learned to use the little bits of time was Abraham Lincoln.

It has been the author's great joy and privilege to be closely associated with young people in school and to watch their habits and struggles in growing into men and women. One great truth is exemplified daily in their lives. Those who do not wait for the study periods, but use the minutes between lunch and class, work algebra problems while waiting for the barber, read the English assignment while waiting in line to receive a football jersey—these are the people who stand at the head of the class. These are the fortunate young who have learned that time is the raw material of life, the chief tool of learning, the basis of individual freedom, and the loom upon which the fabric of work is woven into the tapestry of success.

To appreciate the gift of time you must grow to understand that it is too limited a gift to be wasted in trivialities, hatred, revenge, fault-finding, prejudice, and intolerance and destruction. When you have learned this of time you will be respected for your maturity. But you will also learn that the gift of time is sufficient to absorb and heal your failures, your hurts, your sorrows, your disappointments—but never your shortcomings and weaknesses without vigilance and unceasing help from you. When you have learned this of the gift of time you will be esteemed as one who has developed "a philosophy of life."

The gift of humility

Imagine yourself as an artist. Suppose you decided that you would try to illustrate the thirteen gifts which we are talking about. Some would be rather easy—they could be illustrated by pose or facial expressions. Others would require more complicated expression. But the hardest of all your natural gifts to illustrate would be humility. It is simplicity in spiritual purity, and yet it is found only in greatness of character. What is there in the heroic statue of Lincoln that looks down upon our nation's Capitol from the Lincoln Memorial that radiates out to us the humility of this great character?

In two of the famous creation scenes of Michelangelo on the ceiling of the Sistine Chapel of the Vatican, the artist has done the seemingly impossible. In the scenes of the Creation of Man and God Separating the Waters from the Earth one is struck by the quality of humility that is depicted in the majestic hands of God. How can it be? Is it not perhaps best answered by defining humility in terms new to you? You have probably never thought of humility as power; that is, however, exactly what the gift of humility is. It is the quality opposite to arrogance, and arrogance is weakness. The only power displayed through arrogance is a pretense which results in trampling the beauty of life underfoot, or making association with others unpleasant and something to be avoided.

The gift of humility is so great that it cannot be hidden. The Syrian poet and philosopher, Khalil Gibran, has put it in these words:

When you shall meet one who is strong
and gentle too, pray feast your eyes;
For he is glorious to behold,
The blind can see his qualities.[2]

The gift of humility will make the most single significant contribution to your education and growth, for it is the gift that makes you teachable. It is that gift which makes you a follower, one willing to listen and to accept direction and correction. Wisdom is attained only by those who are teachable, and the greatest stumbling block to being teachable is human pride. This is another name for self-centeredness, which walls the individual about with a shell of resistance, admitting neither recognition of error nor direction for a better way to proceed. The people who learn and grow are those who are ready to listen, who are not afraid to ask questions, who are alert to new ways of doing things, and who accept suggestions for improvement with enthusiasm. These are the people who seem always eager for a new idea, who never profess to know the last answer on any topic, but with refreshing humility find out all they can and put ideas together and convert them into wise judgments.

"Wisdom," says an Oriental proverb, "is no magic formula. It is merely an open and humble mind, constantly thirsting for the fountains of knowledge and

[2]Khalil Gibran, *The Procession* (New York: The Philosophical Library, 1958).

understanding. Its foundations are embedded in a confidence that can only be labelled spiritual." Those qualities which make a leader honored are the same which make a follower sincere. Two thousand years ago a humble teacher said, "Whosoever would be great among you will be your servant." Use the gift of humility to make you teachable; only in this can its true meaning come to you.

The gift of work

"Before the gates of excellence the high gods have placed sweat." Thus wrote the Greek poet, Hesiod, in 800 B.C. Dr. Will Osler is considered by many to be the most influential medical teacher since Hippocrates. He taught at the medical schools of McGill, Pennsylvania, Johns Hopkins, and Oxford universities, and wrote a book on medicine, *The Principles and Practice of Medicine*, which is used in medical schools throughout the world and is found in almost every doctor's office.

On October 1, 1903, Dr. Osler delivered a speech in Toronto entitled "The Master-Word in Medicine." Here is part of what he said:

> ***The master-word . . . I purpose to give you in the hope, yes, the full assurance, that some of you will at least lay hold upon it to your profit. Though a little one, the master-word looms large in meaning. It is the***

open sesame to every portal, the great equalizer in the world, the true philosopher's stone which transmutes all the base metal of humanity into gold. The stupid man among you it will make bright, the bright man brilliant, and the brilliant student steady. With the magic word in your heart all things are possible, and without it all study is vanity and vexation. . . . Not only has it been the touchstone of progress, but it is the measure of success in everyday life. . . . And the master word is **work**, ***a little one, as I have said, but fraught with momentous consequences if you but write it on the tables of your heart, and bind it upon your forehead.***[3]

"Nothing great," said Emerson, "was ever achieved without enthusiasm." If you are enthusiastic about the gifts which are available to you, others will grow around them: character, prudence, common sense, opportunity, discipline, success, discretion, and happiness. These are a treasury of gifts greater than those

[3]Adapted from Dr. Harvey Cushing's *Life of Sir William Osler* (New York: Oxford University Press, 1940).

to be found at the end of a thousand rainbows. If you believe in your star, it will guide you. If you work, you will succeed. If you do your work well, you will enjoy it. The greatest enemy to your chance to improve your grades, to your success in college, to your search for the happy life, is to allow yourself to think that you have developed your gifts and talents enough. Napoleon said, "Life gives the implements to those who can handle them." Let's see what you can do to handle the implements of study more successfully and improve your grades with less drudgery.

CHAPTER 2

Listening: The Easy Way to Learn

The most difficult of all learning processes

It is paradoxical that the ability to listen in the classroom is the easiest of all ways to learn, yet learning to listen is the hardest of all the learning processes to master. Because it is the most difficult for a teacher to teach, it must be almost wholly self-taught. It is the least susceptible to discipline and is seldom accomplished except by the very few, but lack of the ability often makes the bore, so well defined by Ambrose Bierce, "A person who talks when you wish him to listen."

Why is listening the most difficult of the learning processes? The learning processes of seeing (reading), writing, and thinking are exercised within the person. But listening requires the listener to coordinate his mental powers with an outside force—the person or thing to which the listener is listening. This demands the discipline of subjecting the mind of the listener to that of the speaker.

The second problem in learning to listen arises from lack of associated control. When you learn to read, your eyes control the speed with which you read. When you write there is actual physical control in your hand. In thinking the analysis of thought travels at exactly the speed capacity of your mind. But when you begin to train yourself to be a good listener, you are faced with a difficulty not unlike that of trying to drive a car without brakes. You can think four times as fast as the average teacher can speak. Only by demanding of yourself the most unswerving concentration and discipline can you hold your mind on the track of the speaker. This can be accomplished if the listener uses his free time to think around the topic—"listening between the lines" as it is sometimes called. It consists of anticipating the teacher's next point, summarizing what has been said, questioning in silence the accuracy or importance of what is being taught, putting the teacher's thoughts into one's own words, and trying to discern the test or examination questions which will be formed from this material. If you can train yourself to do this you will (1) save yourself much precious time by not having to read what has already been taught; and (2) you can give a more thoughtful and acceptable answer either in oral recitation or on a written test.

When you have learned to adjust your speed of thinking to the rate of a speaker, you have added two valuable elements to your character: (1) ability to discipline your mind to the present; and (2) you have made yourself a follower. Your mind performs in time, but it tries desperately to steer your thoughts into the pleasant, relaxing, reverie of past time; or toward the freedom of unlimited speculation and dreams which the future provides.

Learning to follow a leader

Perhaps you have not found it difficult to follow the captain of a team, the leader of your social group, or the mutually accepted director of your immediate circle of friends. This accepted leadership stems from common interest and mutual understanding. Learning to listen is learning to be a good follower, but in a totally different set of circumstances. First, there is the natural opposition between youth and age. You have great respect and love for your parents, your teachers, and your adult friends, but you cannot always agree that their ways of doing things and their approach to problems are the best ways for you. Your parents want you to listen in order that you may be saved from many of the experiences which they were forced to learn "the hard way"; because they, like you, felt "misunderstood" and closed their minds when they were asked to become followers. Your teacher is talking about the problem on the blackboard, the passage in the textbook, the questions which are asked on examinations, because the experiences of others have demonstrated that help in these particular areas is essential to success.

It takes the very best that you have—mentally and spiritually—to become the follower necessary to be a good listener. Many of your natural gifts must be put to work. First, however, you must convince yourself that you can improve your ability to listen. Then you must accept with enthusiasm, conviction, and common sense the best testing ground available to you, which is, of course, the classroom. Here you must accept the teacher as the leader and attune your ears and your mind to the opportunities which make learning easier and provide a greater degree of success in your school subjects.

The problem of tradition

The fourth stumbling block that stands in the way of those who would become good listeners is tradition. Until recently, within your own lifetime, listening was accepted as a state of mind rather than as a process of learning. Hours and years were spent teaching you to read, and you accepted it as basic to your future learning and success in school. Today, with the vast increase in the content demands of school subjects, plus the use of sound laboratories for languages, and audiovisual methods, you now spend three times as much time listening as you do reading. Finding yourself in this situation is probably a bit puzzling. It might be even more puzzling to realize that during all your years in school you remember no more direction in listening than "Pay attention," or "Sit up and listen"; but you can overcome the tradition of listening as a state of mind, "listening with one's ears," and train yourself to be a good listener.

The distortions that arise from poor listening sometimes cause serious misunderstandings and make effective communication impossible. Sometimes they are amusing, but even these tend to show how little is heard or how easily it becomes something entirely different as it passes from one poor listener to another. One such distortion concerns the words shouted by John Wilkes Booth after murdering Abraham Lincoln in Ford's Theater on the night of April 14, 1865. History has understood the words to be "Sic semper tyrannis," the state motto of Virginia. But a flagman on the Chicago, Aurora and Elgin Railroad gave Carl Sandburg another version. He had heard it differently: "This man Booth," said the flagman, "he shot the Prisidint, jumped down onto the stage and hallooed, 'I'm sick, send for McGinnis!' "

Few do but many can

Although psychologists and communication experts agree that only a minority ever accomplish the art of listening, they point to a much brighter future. Because everyone assumes the ability to listen, it has only been through a series of extensive tests, given after lectures, prepared recordings, and discussions, that research has revealed statistics which attest to the very small percentage of people who have even 50% retention immediately after they have heard something. Experimental courses taught to both student and adult groups have shown that listening is teachable, and can also be self-taught. Many people have been able to double their listening proficiency in a few months. Encouraged by such reports, many educators have added listening courses to school curricula. One notable example is the one-year course required of all freshmen at Michigan State University. The course first emphasizes that listening is an active process, not merely the reception of ideas. The workshop material consists of recorded outlines, speeches, simple word lists, and class lectures. Both students and teachers acclaim its success.

The classroom as a proving ground

You can teach yourself to become a good listener. Each of your classrooms provides a practice laboratory. As you enter each, keep in mind the four basic difficulties to overcome: (1) You must coordinate your listening and thinking powers with an outside force. (2) You must adjust to the difference in the speed of your thinking and the speed of the speaker, and this is best accomplished by disciplining the mind to the present and thinking around the subject—called "listening between the lines." (3) You must be willing to follow, for above all else learning to listen is learning to follow a leader with enthusiasm, conviction, and the common sense appraisal that the classroom is the place to learn to listen. (4) You must accept the findings of research and acknowledge listening as an essential and active learning process which utilizes all your mental faculties, rather than follow the erroneous tradition that listening is merely a state of mind and the passive reception of ideas.

In addition to these four important steps to becoming a better listener, a few suggestions for practice inside and outside the classroom are offered. There are also several "don'ts" worthy of your consideration. Before you continue, however, it would be wise to answer the questions that you are asking: But what am I going to get out of all this practice? How much will I be able to raise my grades? Is it really possible to save time by listening in class?

Comparative studies of material given orally in class and that asked for on tests and examinations puts the good listener in the driver's seat, leading the race. In one history course, tape recordings revealed that 80% of the material asked for at testing time had been presented orally by the teacher. Some of the intelligent questions asked by students in the class were almost identical to the questions they saw later on tests. The percentage for science and mathematics classes was even higher. In several cases, demonstrations and associated material had presented the course so thoroughly that the good listener, capable of taking sufficiently detailed notes, could have achieved an honor grade without using either text or source book. Language tests with sections of sight readings fell to about 50% mastery possible from class listening. Measurements of English classes proved difficult because of the points lost for mistakes in the mechanics of writing, but all comparisons of questions dealing with literature interpretation showed that the answers were given in class.

If you still question the chance to improve your grades by improving your ability to listen, try this simple experiment. As the class is being taught write down what you think will be possible test questions. When testing time comes, see how many of your questions appear. If you give it a fair trial, you will need no further convincing.

Here are the practices which will make you better grades in school and a more acceptable person in life; for in school and in life you are listening for growth, to the better person within you, and to the available truth around you with an open mind.

Taking notes: The ultimate key to listening success

Learn to listen with a pencil in your hand. Open your notebook to a clean page or a continuing dated page and be ready to write.

It has already been suggested that you listen for and write down important questions. Then why not also write briefly, and briefly must be emphasized, either in key word, phrase, or sentence form, material which you think will aid you in reviewing and answering questions later. Chapter 6 of this book deals with outlining and summarizing. Perhaps you should refer to it in preparation for beginning serious note-taking. Notes taken in outline form are recommended. They are easy to take; they tend to direct one toward listening for main ideas rather than attractive statements which may or may not contribute to basic knowledge of a subject or aid in remembering it.

The practice of taking notes in outline form also helps you to avoid one of the common mistakes in taking class notes—writing down, or trying to write down, too much. This well-intended but almost totally tragic practice is often called scribblemania. Scribblemania results in a frantic effort to keep up, working furiously and learning almost nothing.

Notes should serve as water to prime the pump, not as a floodtide to sink one. So why not add to your listening ability and your subject knowledge by starting class with pencil ready and notebook open. Take notes in outline form. Write them in permanent form at the first writing. This only takes a little concern and self-discipline. Copying notes over is one of those useless wastes of time, throwing away the very thing notes were meant to save.

Put the speaker's ideas in your own words (as suggested in Chapter 6) and avoid the delays which arise from trying to spell the speaker's unfamiliar words. Notes in your own words will also have more meaning when you review them later. Recall of material covered will also be much easier, for putting notes in your own words has made them your personal knowledge.

Be sure you have information in mind when you take notes. Although they are arranged as topics and subtopics in outline form, topic headings are useless unless they inform. If your notes relate to an incident in history or to a current event, you should briefly include the four w's of information—who, where, when, and why.

Note-taking, like learning to listen, requires practice. Even though you think all the material you need is in the textbook and associated reading, notes taken in class may make the reading easier by indicating those parts which the teacher considers important. Note-taking and listening complement each other. To become a good listener there is no better practice than note-taking. To lighten the burden of study outside of class and to improve your grade at the same time, there is nothing that rewards more than thoughtful, constant, informative note-taking in class.

Listening Aids for the Classroom

1. Make an evaluation of the percentage of subject material taught in class. If the algebra problems

worked as examples or the history assignment explanation will save you an hour's work at home, use this as a personal inducement. The time saved is your premium to be used to enrich your life in other ways, or to merely enjoy the satisfaction of having time to call your own.

2. Accept the responsibility for getting as much out of a class recitation as that which is required from a reading assignment. You expect to get what a book has to offer from your reading, but the poor listener often starts with the attitude that it is the teacher's responsibility to somehow "get the lesson" through to him. It is your responsibility to get through to the speaker and the lesson.
3. Start "small" in order to avoid discouragement. Once you start to give real listening the test, you might find yourself quite disappointed at the little you can hear and retain. Begin by listening for peak words and clue phrases. Peak words are the key words of the rule or explanation. If four important items are mentioned, start your training by getting a peak word from each that will help you later find what you have missed in your book or in some other source. Clue phrases alert you for something important that follows. The teacher will say, "Watch this important step." "Three principal results are." "You will be asked for this later." How to determine what is important and how to remember it is the thing you must keep constantly in mind. The inflection of the teacher's voice, the topic sentence of an explanation, a summary—these are to the good listener what paragraph and section headings are to the good reader.

4. Make your pencil an important part of your training in listening. Write down the peak words. If you cannot follow rapidly enough to write the "three principal results," write the words "results" and "three." Then get them from the teacher at the end of class or from some other source. Taking notes removes what is to be remembered from the realm of the impersonal and makes it a part of you. Surely you know how much easier it is to remember something you have done than that which you have merely heard about.
5. Train yourself to make your listening three dimensional. Listen critically with your ears, thoughtfully with your mind, and understandingly with your eyes. Critically with your ears so that you may note both good and bad from the oral recitation of your fellow students and profit thereby. Thoughtfully with your mind in order to keep your thinking at the proper speed and at the same time build a capacity for judgment. Understandingly with your eyes, watching the teacher closely at all times, and relaying to the teacher your sincerity, your desire to learn, and your acceptance of responsibility. More significant answers have been observed in listening eyes than could ever be written on an examination paper.
6. Use what you have learned from listening to prove your interest to the teacher and improve your grade. If the teacher has given more than the book offers, by all means use it in your answers. Many a teacher, supposing that such was understood, has heard the question, "May we use material from what we heard in class, or do you just want the

answer from the book?" You can be sure that the part of the answer which the teacher will value most is the part you got from listening.

Almost all the stupid, repetitive, and time-wasting activity of the classroom, that robs people of the right to learn, arises from actions of those described by Professor Jacques Barzun as being "afraid to lend their mind to another's thought, as if it would come back to them bruised and bent." Here are a few listening "don'ts" for the classroom:

1. Don't interrupt in the middle of an explanation to say that you don't understand. If you wait until it's finished you will probably have had your question answered without having to ask it.
2. Don't be too fast with a related question. Until you have trained yourself to a degree of efficiency in listening, you will often be embarrassed by finding that it has already been answered.
3. Don't display such impatience to speak, by frantically waving or tilting forward in your desk, as to indicate that the world's future depended upon what you had to say. Before you signal to speak ask yourself, "Is this worth listening to?"—a far more important question than, "Is this worth saying,"
4. Don't clutter up the thought of those who wish to learn with insignificant and worthless contributions. That you saw *Macbeth* on television does not add to the class's knowledge of *Macbeth*. But if the scenery for Act II, Scene III, was unusual, both teacher and class might enjoy a brief description of it.
5. Don't hurry with those deadly phrases, "But I

think" or "But I thought." If you have thought, all will know it when you speak.

6. Don't ever believe that speaking is more important than listening. It was Voltaire who said, "Men employ speech only to conceal their thoughts." And Socrates, one of the world's great philosophers, had the reputation of being the most patient and inquisitive listener in all Athens.

Daily exercises in listening

All the waking hours of the day provide myriad opportunities to improve one's ability to listen. The requests made by parents that go unheard, the sounds of the world around you—the song of a bird, the interesting conversation of the two people seated next to you, the name of the person to whom you have just been introduced. The last is the one almost universal test of a poor listener. You are introduced to Tom McCabe or Joan Banks—simple sounds—yet five minutes later you say, "I'm sorry, but I missed your name." You heard the name with your ears only—your mind was making a critical assessment, your eyes were busy with the color of a jacket or dress, perhaps you were trying to place the person geographically. All these things could have followed the initial listening, but they replaced it instead. Here are some practices which will help you develop your ability to listen outside the classroom.

1. Make a resolution each morning for two weeks that during the day no one will have to repeat a single thing said to you.
2. Practice selectivity. As you go to and from school, or wherever you go, or whatever you are doing,

there are many sounds around you. Practice picking out those you wish to hear. Close your mind to all others. John Kieran, the naturalist, could sit amid cheering thousands at a football game in the heart of New York City and pick out the "honk, honk" of a Canada goose flying south high against the November sky.

3. Start hearing the things you really enjoy. Do you really have to play your new phonograph record a dozen times to learn the words? The answer is "No." Test yourself—you can master the whole song with two playings.
4. Form a team with a friend. Read each other poetry, sports scores, or whatever is of interest, and see what percentage the listener can repeat correctly.
5. Recordings of speeches and literary readings are excellent for self-teaching. They are available at many public libraries.
6. Develop a consciousness for your own speaking so that you will be clearly heard and understood. This will make a profound indirect contribution to your own listening ability.

CHAPTER 3

The Classroom: Atmosphere for Achievement

Partnership with the teacher

Listening is an important part of classroom success, but many other elements contribute to giving the classroom an atmosphere for achievement, or making it a wasteland of indifference and futility. The contribution that you make toward maintaining an environment of learning will determine to no small degree what your mark will be. If you are to succeed there must be a continuous and effective partnership between you and your teachers.

Two simple tests can give you a sound estimate of how profitable this partnership is in your own case. First, make an estimate of what the class would be like if all the people in it acted and responded in the same way as you do. Would there be a general air of indifference and inattention, or would a sense of responsibility and willingness to learn prevail? Would the class time be taken up with stupid questions and excuses for not being able to recite, or would intelligent discussion and well-organized recitation contribute much to all? It is important that this partnership be effective and produce the proper results. It is in fact the greatest enterprise of your life. Your education, or lack of it, will make possible, or limit, opportunity and success for the remainder of your life.

Now examine the strength or weakness of this important joint venture by the second test: put yourself in the teacher's place. Is your work the quality that you would like if you were the teacher? Do you respond to correction and help as you yourself would like? If you were the teacher would you pick yourself as one of the most diligent and cooperative members of the class? You may not be the smartest person in the class, but you can be the most responsive and appreciative.

Every teacher knows that he or she is not teaching to all the people in any given class. Some are there for the social ride, some because their parents require it, some because the state is willing to spend money to buy something precious for somebody who won't accept it, and some are there because they want to learn. If you were the teacher, in which of the groups would you place yourself? And if you were the teacher, one of the most complimentary things you could ever say about one of your students would be, "He wants to learn." What do your teachers say of you?

Practices for classroom efficiency

1. Adopt the proper point of view. Although we are gregarious by nature, expecting the classroom to be a social activity will result in disappointment.

Learning is not a social affair, but a very lonely business. Even in the midst of people, learning produces loneliness—and the greater the learning, the greater the loneliness. It is not fun. Learning anything of value is difficult. It is hard and tedious work, often exasperating and discouraging. It has moments of joy and exhilaration which arise from the warm inward feeling of achievement; and the kindness of a good teacher who through understanding and appreciation, but never by diminishing requirements, is able to make the task less difficult and less painful. The teachers you remember with gratitude are the ones who require of you the greatest degree of excellence, and never compromise the real purpose of the classroom by trying to disguise it behind a social front of meaningless give-and-take or the absurdity of baseless argument.

2. Go to class prepared. The two commonly required preparations are written work and oral recitation. If a written assignment is required as homework, form the habit of judging it by three questions: (1) Am I pleased with it? (2) Will it satisfy my teacher? (3) Will it stand in competition for effort as the number one paper in the class? If it is an oral recitation, you may also evaluate the extent of your preparation by three questions: (1) Is my knowledge sufficient to make a positive contribution to classroom discussion? (2) Have I an intelligent design for answers to direct questions? (3) How will my oral recitation be judged by other members of the class and the teacher?

   Am I pleased with my written assignment? The

term format is applied to the form a paper takes—location of your name, indentation, spacing of problems or sentences, numbering for easy location by the teacher, proportion and sensible arrangement for marking. It is so futile to present work that will identify you as a sloppy, indifferent student. Your name is your trademark. Yet how many students scribble it illegibly across a paper? If your paper lacks form, neatness, and completeness, and you are sufficiently content to pass it in, you are putting yourself on record as one lacking in self-respect, willing to deal in mediocrity, whose sole ambitious aim is to get by.

Will my written assignment satisfy the teacher? Have I followed the specific directions given with the assignment? Even though I was not able to solve two of the problems, or translate three of the sentences, does my paper reflect sufficient responsibility and effort to show my desire to do the very best of which I am capable? If I were the teacher would I be satisfied with this paper? Would I write "Good" at the end of it or would I write "Insufficient effort"?

Will my written assignment stand in competition for effort as the number one paper in the class? Others may have more mastery of the subject, but your teacher learns very quickly your capabilities. You may miss half the answers and get a mark of 50, but no one can prevent you from making a 100 in effort. This same effort is a great booster of marks.

Turning to oral recitation, it might be worth restating what is common knowledge among all good teachers: oral recitation can be a most exciting and profitable way to learn. It can also be a total farce and a complete waste of time. How do you classify yourself as a participant in oral recitation? There are usually some of each of the following types in every class: (1) The unprepared bluffer—this person attempts to cover up his ignorance by asking unrelated questions or volunteering unreliable information gathered from comic books and movies. (2) The Epimethean critic—this person gets his title from Epimetheus, the Greek god who possessed only hindsight, while his brother, Prometheus, the benefactor of mankind, possessed foresight. In class the Epimethean critic might listen to the reading of a perfectly beautiful poem, but he can never resist the time-destroying speculation as to why it wasn't written another way, or "Why wouldn't it have been better if—?" Although his glance is always backward, he will not accept the judgment of either history or time-proven authority. (3) The fluttering magpie—if you have attended the aviary at a zoo you probably remember that the one bird that could remain neither still nor quiet was the magpie. This type interrupts constantly, always before he has given any thought to what he is going to say. More often than not he repeats something inadequately that has already been stated clearly and thoroughly. (4) The sensitive hopeful—this person has prepared sufficiently to recite, but is afraid of what the teacher and other students will think of the recitation. The organization that will be suggested for question two in reference to oral recitation will help this type overcome his fear. (5) The accomplished leader—this student prepared his assignment, recited the essentials to himself, and established a point of view for possible oral discussion and a frame upon which to hang the answers to questions asked.

What answers do you need for the three questions evaluating oral recitation to separate you from all categories of oral performers except number five? Is my knowledge sufficient to make a positive contribution to classroom discussion? Since most teachers follow the textbook closely, it is not difficult to predict what will be discussed in class. If you fear oral recitation, begin by anticipating one or two topics which you think likely for discussion. A chance to recite on these will help dispel fear. You will also learn that a sincere and honest recitation is not met by critical judgments. A little inquiry will probably also reveal that you are not the only responsible student who fears reciting; only the bore and the clown operate brazenly.

Have I an intelligent design for answers to direct questions? Make the frame for your answer affirmative rather than negative. Do not start your answer by questioning the truth of your own statement. To begin with "Isn't it true?" or "Doesn't the book say?" casts doubt even before you have stated your point. Other "don'ts" include such introductions as "I don't know but," "I heard or read somewhere," "It seems to me," and "I'm not sure but I think."

Design your answer to give your listeners assurance that you know what you are talking about. Try to make a quick blueprint before you start, particularly as to how you will end your answer. A painful experience for others is to see a splendid answer shredded by "and" phrases and insignificant details merely because the person reciting has not anticipated a climax and quick closing. Imagine your recitation as a one-minute drama which is to be properly staged; or that for the period of your individual recitation you are the director of the meeting, controlling your audience and speaking so clearly that everyone will understand. If you so design, the third question will have been answered—you will be judged by teacher and students to belong in the group of "accomplished leaders."

"And all this," you say, "for nothing more important than participating orally in class!" Yes, all this and more.

3. Go to class with the proper tools. Most important is your textbook. The student who enters class without his book is revealing lack of interest as flagrantly as if he wore a large placard inscribed I HAVE NO INTEREST IN THIS CLASS. A well-sharpened pencil, a pen, a notebook with paper for writing, an assignment book for recording assignments, a ruler, protractor, and compass for mathematics, all should be ready for immediate use. Neither the teacher nor your fellow students will long respect a chronic borrower. Besides, it is your responsibility to go to class equipped for efficient work, and not to do so is gross neglect and lack of preparation. If you were playing cen-

ter field, and inning after inning went out without your glove, do you think the coach would keep you on the team very long? Imagine going to your music lesson and forgetting to take your trumpet or violin. Arriving in class without the tools will very quickly put you off the team and out of the lesson.

4. Follow classroom instructions. One of the most tragic of all student faults is not paying attention to assignments. When the teacher makes an assignment, write it down. Have a special notebook or a division of your general notebook, and be the first with a pencil when the teacher starts to give the assignment. The teacher, scanning the room, quickly recognizes the irresponsible Joes and Janes who will waste time telephoning later, or will do the wrong assignment, or nothing at all.

   Certain instructions are given which the teacher expects to be carried out during the entire course. If you are asked to skip a line between answers, number sentences on the left side of the red margin, leave one inch indentation on the right side of your paper, not to fold papers, put your name in the upper right corner—don't forget after a week and put your name in the upper left.

   Write down the general operating instructions for each class when they are given. Keep them in the front of your notebook for quick reference. Your teacher has worked out an efficient system to expedite his own work and bring order into yours. Never affront him or her with such baseless barbarism as, "But I've always done it this way."

That is probably the best possible reason for his or her way.

Accepting classroom instructions and following them puts you in the "atmosphere for achievement." Good habits are as easy to follow as bad ones. The bad ones produce bad grades; the good ones produce good grades. Nothing could be simpler than this. It becomes a matter of choice. Choose wisely.

5. Study the implications of questions before you ask them. The teacher learns much from the nature of the questions you ask about your work. If you are assigned a composition to write, don't ask, "How long does it have to be?" Ask instead, "What do you wish us to include?" If you are assigned a report to bring to class, do not ask, "Why do we have to do this?" It is more helpful to ask, "Where can I find the best reference material?" One of the most glaring of all negative approaches is to look at a test paper, then without checking answers against your book, walk up to the teacher and ask, "Why'd you mark me off on this?" First check your answer against the book, then give your question positive and concerned implication by asking, "Did I not explain thoroughly enough?" or "What other material would have made a better answer?" The basic difference lies in "Why do I?" or "Why'd you?" and "How can I?" and "Did I not?" One produces nothing, the other results in sympathetic help and mutual understanding.
6. Practice good classroom manners. Nothing can destroy the rapport of student and teacher so quick-

ly, or permanently damage their essential partnership, as bad classroom manners and the absence of any effort toward improvement. Arrive in class on time and do not start looking at your watch halfway through the period. Do not start putting on your jacket and gathering up your books five minutes before the period ends. Important information is sometimes given toward the end of class. Besides, what would a coach think of a player who slacked off before the game was over? The way you carry your books (and the wise student carries them in a briefcase), your posture as you sit at your desk or stand to recite, the manner in which you enter and leave the classroom—all these are either detrimental to or make a contribution to the "atmosphere for achievement."

Classroom efficiency is the product of self-respect, cooperation, and a willingness to learn. When you approach the teacher's desk to ask a question, stand erect, keep your hands by your side, and never lean over and put your hands on the desk. Coordinate your classroom manners to the methods of the teacher. If the teacher asks that questions be saved until the end of the period, do not interrupt in the middle. When you are late to class, be courteous enough to explain why at the end of the class. If you are absent from class, show enough concern to ask the teacher if you missed anything which you should get from someone who was present.

A little observation will reveal that the best students are those who maintain a high standard of classroom manners. They are aware that what is being done in the classroom is to help them learn. They are conscious of the continuing judgment that the interested and devoted teacher makes. Perhaps, except on isolated occasions, the student's only means of expressing gratitude and appreciation is through courtesy—from which all good classroom manners grow.

CHAPTER 4

Study Time: Design for Success

Time is learning's most important tool

Reference has been made to time as a wonderful gift. The true value of study time can perhaps best be emphasized by an often quoted statement which says: "All genuine learning is self-education." The guidance and self-evaluation which the classroom offers are not to be discounted; however, since we have already admitted that "learning is a lonely business," it is not unreasonable to place premium value upon the time you spend alone in study. The great philosopher-emperor of Rome, Marcus Aurelius, said that "the present is the only thing of which a man can be deprived." And the Greek philosopher, Epicurus, pointed out that we ourselves are the deprivers: "But you, who are not master of tomorrow, postpone your happiness: life is wasted in procrastination." In Chapter 1 reference was made to procrastination as one of the most ruthless destroyers of time. In this chapter more specific and detailed methods for the proper use of "our most limited blessing" will be considered.

Finding where the hours go

The first step toward establishing routine and order in regard to the use of time is an awareness of where your weakness lies and where you must begin the fight. It seems to be universally expressed, whether true or not, that there just isn't enough time. The person who leaves classes at 3 p.m. is sure that he will have no difficulty in finding time to do his assignments before classes start at eight or nine the next morning. At least on the clock there is plenty of time—three hours (3:30–6:30) before dinner and three hours (7:00–10:00) after dinner. Six hours and four assignments, no need to rush, not more than an hour needed for each. "Certainly, I can walk with you to the drugstore. I can play touch football."

And after dinner the news was on television. Then there was a favorite program (just half an hour), or a new magazine had come in the mail. "Where did I leave my books? I think I'll check with a friend to be sure of the history assignment. Now it is 8:45 p.m. and I have to sharpen my pencil. I have sharpened my pencil. Which assignment should I do first? I have glanced at four books in quick succession. I have repiled three of them. The fourth is open in front of me. I just brushed some dandruff off my sweater. I must look in the mirror to see whether or not my dandruff isn't getting worse."

It is now 9:10 p.m. The next morning, fifteen minutes before the first class, there is a last hopeless and futile attempt to cram into a few minutes what had once had hours for completion. Then is heard the oft-repeated lament—"there just isn't enough time."

This account of frittering away the hours is a pattern, with variations, that is enacted daily. Wishful thinking is a deep-seated human trait which carries us along the line of least resistance. It takes courage and action to face up boldly to how we use or abuse our time. So the first step toward the proper organization of time for better use is to find out what you are doing with your time at present.

Self-discovery and self-evaluation are the only really effective means of convincing yourself of where your time goes. Make a time chart of your waking hours and for one week, being completely honest with yourself, record in as much detail as possible what you do. A simple notebook size chart, which may be conveniently kept in the front of your notebook, might be made as follows.

How to make a schedule

Do the same for each day of the week. At the end of the week make a total for the entire week. Do not be embarrassed by your findings. Be convinced that you can rearrange and reallot your time to greater advantage. If one week's trial does not convince you, carry the experiment through a second or third week.

Psychologists and efficiency experts have done much research in the advantage of organized time. The results of this research show the tremendous value in time saving. They show the effectiveness of work approached with a definite job in mind rather than the question "What next?" as is the approach of many students to their studies. Research has shown that the

TIME USE CHART
Monday, September 5

Hours	
A.M.	Arrived at school 8:30
8–9	Talked with friends 8:30–9
9–10	Chemistry class
10–11	Study period. Went to school library, read magazine.
11–12	History class
P.M.	Lunch for half hour
12–1	Cannot remember what I did until 1 p.m.
1–2	English class
2–3	Math class
	3–3:30 travel home
3–4	3:30–4 snack, telephone, etc.
4–5	Met friend at drugstore
5–6	Read English assignment 15 min. Listened to records.
6–7	Dinner
7–8	
8–9	
9–10	

TOTALS—12 hours (excepting two for meals)

Time in class	4
Time studying outside of class	....
Time in social activity and recreation (talking, drugstore, telephone, records, etc.)	....
Time otherwise accounted for	....
Time not accounted for	....

energy saved through good organization is directed toward the job at hand. Consequently, one of the significant benefits of organization, system, and a well-planned schedule for study is the power that organization makes available.

It is interesting to note from the same surveys that students who have part-time jobs, either in the afternoons or on weekends, manage to find more study time than those who have nothing in the nature of definite time responsibility. The student who is paid for two hours of his labor has learned that time has value—dollars and cents value. At the place of afternoon employment he is required to start at 3:30. He can't decide to do something else until 4; thus he receives basic training in working by a schedule. Having less time for study probably forces him to budget his time more accurately than those with more time. Whatever the reasons, the results are the same. In almost every case the person with less time available found more time for study and made better grades.

If you have not convinced yourself of the value of plan and organization for the use of time, listen to a noted psychologist, Dr. B. C. Ewer:

If we have several duties confronting us simultaneously, it is only too likely that we shall fail to do any of them. They seem to get in each other's way. The pressure of each prevents us from giving ourselves whole-heartedly to any, or we turn in futile fashion from one to another, dropping each as soon as it is begun.

The title of this chapter, "Study Time: Design for Success," contains a magic word—*Design.* How then shall you design your time in order to avoid all the problems noted above, use your capacities to better advantage with less strain, and improve your grades? There are two possible designs. You can buy the first design ready-made in the form of a plan book. It might have the title Teacher's Plan Book, but do not let this disturb you. The Milton Bradley Plan Book is available from the Milton Bradley Company, Springfield, Massachusetts. Your teachers would probably be able to recommend others equally as good. The days of the week are divided into enough periods to take care of your classes and study periods, with space left over for afternoon and evening planning. A week's schedule would be approximately six times larger than our model; each space would be large enough to write in assignments or what to study. Classes and study periods are filled in to indicate how your completed schedule might look. The assignment can be included with each class. That is one advantage of a plan book which is divided into thirty weeks and covers the entire school year.

The approximate size of each period would be as follows:

Monday
Math
Pages 1–5
Exercise 2
Problems 1–8

There is sufficient space for recording the assignment skeleton; however, details would be written in your regular notebook. Some students prefer a work schedule without any assignment space. One copy of such a schedule in the front of your notebook and another copy posted on the wall by your study desk would suffice, perhaps with minor changes, for the entire school year. Such a schedule is usually divided into twelve working hours between 8 a.m. and 10 p.m., with an hour each for lunch and dinner.

Subject Period Time	Monday	Tuesday	Wednesday	Thursday	Friday	Saturday
Math. I 9–10	*Math* Pages 1–5 Exercise 2 Problems 1–8	*Math*	*Math*	*Math*	*Math*	
English II 10–11	*English* Julius Caes. Act I Pages 1–34	*English*	*English*	*English*	*English*	French for Monday
Study III 11–12	*Study* Math. for Tuesday	*Study* Math. for Wednesday	*Study* Math. for Thursday	*Study* Math. for Friday	*Study* Math. for Monday	History for Monday
French IV 1–2	*French* Review Exer. Vocab. p. 10	*French*	*French*	*French*	*French*	
History V 2–3	*History* Problems in Democracy Pages 5–17	*History*	*History*	*History*	*History*	
End of School						

3–3:30	Band Prac.	Band Prac.	Band Prac.	Band Prac.	Band Prac.	
3:30–4	Going home					
4–5	Exercise Recreation	Same	Same	Same	Same	
5–6	Study French				Study French for Monday	
7–8	Study History					
8–9	Study English					
9–10	Read, Review, Rest					

TIME SCHEDULE

Twelve Hours	Monday	Tuesday	Wednesday	Thursday	Friday	Saturday	Sunday
8–9	8–8:30 Bus to School Review one subject						
9–10	Chemistry Class						
10–11	English Class						
11–12	Study Chem. for Tues.	Study Chem. for Wed.	Study Chem. for Thurs.	Study for Chem. test Friday	Study Chem. for Monday	Study English for Monday	
1–2	Math. Class					Good Study Time	
2–3	History Class						

3–4	Home and Exercise						
4–5	Recreation			Study for Chemistry Test			
5–6	Study Math. for Tues.	Study Math. for Wed.	Study Math. for Thurs.	Study Math. for Fri.	Study Math. for Mon.		
7–8	Study Hist. for Tues.	Study Hist. for Wed.	Study Hist. for Thurs.	Study Hist. for Fri.	Study Hist. for Mon.		
8–9	Study Eng. for Tues.	Study Eng. for Wed.	Study Eng. for Thurs.	Study Eng. for Fri.	Recreation		
9–10	Relax and Read	Listen to Music					
	Comments All work finished	Comments	Comments	Comments	Comments A good week. Grades up.	Comments	Comments

Although there is much to commend each type of schedule, many students prefer one without any assignment space. Only one day, Monday, is filled in fully. Several things are very important if a schedule is to work effectively. Notice that the period from 11 to 12 is used to study the same subject each day. The same is true for 5 to 6, 7 to 8, and 8 to 9. Research has shown that doing the same thing at the same time each day makes the work seem much easier because it does away with the energy-consuming self-conflict and the confusion of deciding "What next?" It becomes a part of you—not an external force with which you have to contend.

The schedule also shows you that much time can be used for the things you want to do—perhaps more than you ever thought available. Saturday and Sunday have been left almost blank, but it is very wise to apportion a sensible amount of time for study and reading. If you have a part-time job, you will probably find it easy to allot this time. Two interesting results have beeen noted from the study of proper time usage. First, the more one has to do the easier it is to make a workable schedule and follow it. Secondly, people who follow a schedule study fewer hours and get better grades than people who do not restrict themselves to allotted time, but kid themselves into believing that they study all the time. The person who works without a schedule is the one who fails a test and then complains, "But I studied three-and-a-half hours." What this person admits is that three-and-a-half hours were spent seated with a book, daydreaming, thinking fuzzy thoughts at the edge of the subject but never really getting into it.

People who follow a schedule of work train themselves to concentrate. Problems in concentration are, in fact, problems in the effective use of time. The person who sets himself a time limit to get a job done makes a choice. He chooses between getting the job done or dreaming in a half-hearted way for an equally indefinite period of time.

The first of all good study habits is the proper use of time. A well-organized schedule, followed until it becomes a natural part of living, brings into existence the second great aid to study—the ability to concentrate. From the combined results of these two come, as quoted from Dr. Osler, "that most precious of all knowledge—the power of work." From "the power of work" and not from wishful thinking or idle dreams, comes the better grades for which you strive.

It is within your power to bring productive and effective order into your life. The suggestions which follow can make a time schedule work for you, and take half the confusion, worry, indecision, and effort out of your study:

Making your schedule work

1. Give your schedule a fair chance. After you have evaluated your loss of time without a schedule and have prepared a working schedule, do not expect procrastination, resistance, and self-deception to disappear at once. A month of diligence and discipline is perhaps the minimum time necessary for developing the habit of going from one activity to study, or from class to study, or from study of one subject to another, without loss of either time or the power of concentration.
2. Put your schedule to work in a definite place. Place is as important as time in making your schedule

work. If you study in a study hall or the library at school, always sit at the same desk or table. Have what you need—pencils, paper, books—when you sit down, and discipline yourself not to move until a certain block of work has been finished. If you study at home, study in your room at an uncluttered, well-lighted desk that does not face the window. Put all distractions out of reach and sight if possible. Your friend's picture, magazines, or unanswered letters will pull you away and waste your time because you will lose your power of concentration.

If it is noisy at home, study in the public library. The library offers the best atmosphere for study; the setting, the quiet, the presence of books and other people deep in concentration will all help you put your schedule into effect.

Do not kid yourself by thinking that you can study and listen to music, catch snatches of television, or listen to people talk. It cannot be done, and this has been proved by numerous tests and experiments. There is no common ground where study, relaxation, and sociability meet. There is a place for study and a place for relaxation and sociability. If you attempt to make them the same, your study schedule will never work.

3. Study the same thing at the same time each day. This further strengthens the good habit of action by second nature. It also eliminates the exception—always troublesome and causing some delay. You are prepared mentally for that which you are used to doing with regularity. Mental preparation is the first step toward concentration.
4. Fit your schedule to your needs. You know your

capacities. One subject will take you longer than another. Learn to measure your concentration span. If you can only work effectively for half an hour, plan your schedule with a five-minute rest period to take your eyes and mind off the work before you.

5. Do not be too heroic in making your first schedule. If you make yourself into a relentless "grind" for two weeks, you might find a schedule so thoroughly distasteful that you will never try it long enough to appreciate its true purpose: to make your work easier and to provide you with freedom, not to sentence you to constant drudgery.
6. Do not be afraid to change your schedule to take care of emergencies and recurring natural variations that arise.

A very important part of your education is to learn to judge between conflicting interests. When changes occur try to keep the pattern of the day and week as nearly regular as possible. All changes must be followed through to their conclusions. For example, on the model schedule, if you decide to play basketball on Thursday afternoon between 4 and 5, you must allot time to study for the chemistry test. Not to do so is to defeat the purpose of the schedule, which is to provide you with the time you need to study for the chemistry test.

A time schedule is a design for success, both in school and in life. The work habits of the people who have achieved success invariably show a well-designed work pattern. These people make their schedule of accomplishment one of the chief responsibilities of their lives. If you aim at success in school and in life, you can do no less.

CHAPTER 5

Mastering Assignments: Methods of Study

Study methods and the individual

When the climate of study has been created, the time allotted, and the assignment before you, methods of attack are next in order. These are the habits of study which must be practiced until they, like the proper use of time, become a natural part of your life—as natural as the daily habits of dressing, eating, or reading the newspaper.

Methods of study will, of course, require modification and adjustment from one course to the next. For example, the methods used to learn mathematics are somewhat different from those used in studying history, but the basic principles of study are adaptable to all courses.

The individuality of each person also determines to a large degree how one or another of the methods can best be used. Regarding study methods, the mind performs four functions in varying degrees of proficiency. These functions are (1) receiving—through your gift of perception; (2) classifying—by your gift of judgment (thought); (3) preserving—laying away through your gift of memory; (4) recalling—bringing back for use the impressions you have stored away. Remembering these four functions and frequently estimating the effectiveness of each in your own study habits will enable you to discover your capacities and limitations in each area. Knowing how your own mind works is essential if you are to adopt study habits which will best serve you. From this understanding comes the self-confidence needed to achieve excellence.

You can never fully understand and appreciate your wonderful mind. It operates in two areas—the conscious and the subconscious. The functions of preserving and recalling use both the conscious and the subconscious. Impressions not in immediate use are stored away in the subconscious. Although little is understood of how it is done, you can train your subconscious mind to store carefully, so that recall will respond quickly to association or will.

It has been estimated that probably only about 10% of our daily mental activity takes place in the area of the conscious. Behind every conscious act lies the influence of the subconscious. A vast collection of ideas, impressions, and feelings are at work, constituting perhaps 90% of our mental activity. It is therefore important to the development of good study methods to be aware of the mysterious, yet working, subconscious area of the mind. Psychologists generally agree that we really never forget. This in itself should be cause for gratification, for you, like most of us, probably complain often about forgetting. Much of what is labeled as forgotten was never known. You looked at the French vocabulary, but your mind was recording the impression of plans you had for the weekend. Once something is impressed upon your mind, it may become obscured from lack of use, but it is never totally lost. In response to your will or to an association it can be recalled. Perhaps there is no better time and place than the present to resolve to use your will power with greater awareness to preserve that which you learn in a more orderly manner. You can also aid all functions of the mind by resisting the overworked excuse, "But I forgot." Change it to a positive and determined inquiry, "Did I really know in the first place?"

Once you become aware of the functions which the mind performs in learning, one further observation will help you approach study methods from a vantage point missed by many. This observation deals with "aptitude," a word frequently misused in connection with learning. The mistaken ideas circulated during the past few years plus the prevalence of numerous aptitude tests have caused many students to conclude that in some subjects they are void of aptitude and therefore progress is impossible.

The myth of aptitude

People are born with varying degrees of power to learn, but no one inherits aptitudes. Aptitudes result from how the power to learn is applied. A child who becomes interested in music may use his power to learn so successfully that he becomes an accomplished musician at a very early age. The quality of genius rests mainly in the power to learn. When someone is called precocious, it is the ability to learn that sets him apart—not inherited aptitudes. Do not assume inability because you have given lack of interest a more acceptable name—lack of aptitude. Has it not occurred to you that the more you know about a subject the more aptitude you admit? Just because we do not like something enough to concentrate our effort upon it does not prove lack of aptitude. If you are going to truly educate yourself, you will find it necessary to develop interest in many subjects which you think you do not like, and indeed which you might not like. T. S. Eliot put it this way: "No one can become really educated without having pursued some study in which he took no interest—for it is a part of education to learn to interest ourselves in subjects for which we have no aptitude." He could have added that when we have interested ourselves sufficiently to learn about a subject, we find to our surprise that we do have the aptitude.

Psychological research has not yet been able to separate interest and aptitude. Until such is the case do not flaunt the phrase, "I have no aptitude" too freely. It might be an admission which you would just as soon not make public. Mental potential may be generally established at birth, but our power to learn and to develop our special abilities can be constantly improved by learning habits which we set for ourselves.

Variations of the basic methods

All methods of study stem from the three basic skills of learning: (1) finding what you want; (2)

fixing it in your mind; (3) applying it successfully. You will notice little difference in some of the methods which follow. It would be wise to study them closely and to try each before you adopt any one for all or some of your subjects. One method might prove excellent for algebra but poor for history. Fit the method to the subject and to your own natural inclinations. Three items occur in all the methods; they are (1) read, (2) question, and (3) recite. With slight modifications, as to approach, you will note that these constitute the principal ingredients of all good study habits.

One method widely recommended is the 4 *S* = *M* formula. The formula means Four Steps = Mastery. The four steps in mastering the assignment are (1) the preliminary survey; (2) reading the assignment for ideas and converting each paragraph, section, definition, etc. into questions; (3) the quick review—rereading those paragraphs, rules, and definitions which you do not recall at a quick glance; (4) summarizing the material studied briefly and logically in your mind.

The preliminary survey requires less time than any of the other three steps. When done properly it can prove of great value. The first step in the preliminary survey of any assignment is to recall yesterday's lesson and associate the two. This is important because most subject matter leads toward an understanding of a unit or block of material.

The second part of the preliminary survey in reading assignments such as English, history, or science texts, is to check chapter title, section headings, and paragraph headings in italics or boldface. The second step for mathematics and language assignments is to read carefully all rules, definitions, and instructions, and apply them to examples or sample translations.

The third step of the preliminary survey for all types of assignments is the question, "What can I use from yesterday's assignment to help me with this one?" One rule, one definition, or one classroom interpretation can save precious time if remembered before the work actually begins.

A fourth step may be used if a reading assignment is a complete chapter. Some books provide introductory and summary paragraphs which are invaluable in making the chapter's contents clear. Get to know your books, and if such paragraphs are included, read them carefully as the fourth step in your preliminary survey.

The preliminary survey for reading assignments will usually take between five and seven minutes. It will take from ten to twenty minutes for language and mathematics; however, if done properly it will cut much more than that from the time needed to work the problems or write the exercises.

Because young people often hear adult advice with skepticism, test results might be convincing. Two hundred students, representing various high school subjects, were separated into two groups of one hundred each. One group was taught to use the preliminary survey as the first step in studying an assignment. Each group was clocked for the length of time used for study, and each group was given identical tests on the material studied. The group using the preliminary survey was found to study 30% less and average seven points higher when tested. Individual tests from within the same groups showed that some individuals who used the preliminary survey had more comprehension of the material than some who read through the entire assignment without it. It took these students forty minutes to complete the assignment; ten were required for the preliminary survey.

The second step toward mastery, reading the assignment for ideas and converting small units into questions, contains three very important words: (1) reading, (2) ideas, and (3) questions. Reading as used here means concentrating, remembering, and applying —the primary aims of all good readers. Of the three methods of reading—(1) skimming, (2) careful, and (3) intensive—the method used here is intensive reading—reading to be understood clearly and remembered for application.

To read for *ideas* requires the reader to see groups of words rather than single words. Very few ideas are expressed in single words. Note this sentence: Learning how to study requires much self-discipline over a long period of time. There are thirteen words in the sentence. The single-word reader will miss the three ideas: (1) Learning how to study requires something —what? (2) Much self-discipline—under what circumstances? (3) A long period of time. One need not ponder how much easier it is to remember three things instead of thirteen.

Reading for *ideas* leads naturally to the *questions*, as shown by the question that each of the above ideas fosters. An accumulation of ideas in a paragraph, section, or definition immediately becomes a question for the reader who has trained himself in this very important study habit. It is the formation of the question that most helps the mind's functions of laying away for future use and recalling when application is desired. In most assignments, application is almost always in the form of answering *questions* in class—the questions you have formed while studying, if you have chosen wisely.

The quick review, step number three in the mastery of an assignment, is beneficial not only to check against incomplete preparation, but also provides excellent training for increasing one's speed in reading, recall, and comprehension. The method of reading used for the quick review is *skimming*—fast reading to check or find a particular thing. When skimming reveals parts not recalled, the reader will return to intensive reading. One aim of all good study habits is to work more effectively within a limited time. The student should use the third step in assignment mastery to gain speed. In fact, to go back over material at a snail's pace is likely to lessen the power of concentration and produce confusion rather than clarification.

The fourth step in mastery of the assignment—summarizing the material briefly and logically—has sometimes been referred to as "wrapping up the package." This is an apt description for by this step you prepare your goods for presentation in the classroom. Summary writing and outlining are covered in detail in the next chapter. Both can be used effectively in mastering your work.

Much can also be gained through oral summarization—a mental blueprint. Form your mental picture from these logical elements: (1) What the assignment encompasses—that is, its dimensions—beginning and end. (2) The steps or order by which it moves—how one topic or rule leads to the next. (3) The proper judgment in choosing key ideas—ideas which will aid in recalling peripheral ideas if they are needed. (4) What was this assignment designed to teach—can its message or meaning be put in a single statement?

"But," you say, "all these steps and questions will take so long. Besides, I always read my assignments three times. Sometimes I study one assignment two or three hours."

You can only be reminded that good methods of study are designed to shorten the time you need for study and allow you to accomplish more in less time. You may also remind yourself that all reading is not study, and that sitting with a book in your hands is not necessarily reading. Sometimes it is dreaming.

Perhaps you would like to try a formula which is slightly different from the one just discussed. Dr. Francis P. Robinson suggests a brief survey to locate core ideas, followed by the *Q 3 R* method of study.[1]

The *Q* represents question. After you have made the brief survey you should ask the master question—What am I going to learn? Many students fail to prepare their minds psychologically to learn by omitting this valuable yet simple beginning.

The *Q 3 R* formula puts the questions before the reading. The section and paragraph headings are possible starting points for the questions. Turn the headings into a question and then read to answer your question. Questions can be formed from sources other than headings and skill in formulating the right questions can be developed. Training in question formula-

[1]Francis P. Robinson, *Effective Study* (New York: Harper and Bros., 1946).

tion should begin in the classroom. Note the type of question the teacher asks and look for clues to similar questions in your textbook. Topic sentences provide clues. Numbered material—the three reasons, the four results, the two exceptions—are dead giveaways for questions. Use numbered items to form your questions. If the textbook has end-of-chapter questions, these may be used for practice by comparing them to the content they represent, but remember that few teachers rely entirely on such questions.

To make this method of study effective you must first learn to judge how large a section of the assignment you can make questions for; then read without losing your questions. The question should arouse your interest so that as you read, comprehension comes much more easily. Formulating questions before you read also introduces main points with more clarity. Forming good questions and reading to answer them demands much conscientious effort and practice. The proof of its value comes when you see your questions on the daily quiz or the weekly test.

Experiments with a group of high school freshmen at Kent School, in which they kept a written record of their questions, showed that after six weeks' practice, 80% of all classroom questions were being anticipated and prepared. Experiments at the same school, and with juniors in several public high schools, showed that students given the formula with the *Q* omitted averaged nine points less on identical tests than students using the whole formula.

The 3 *R* of the formula stands for read, recite, and review. After the questions have been formed on the paragraph, section, or block of material that can be handled, the reading is done for one thing only—to answer the questions. After you have read to answer the questions, look away from the book and repeat the answers. This accomplishes the second *R* of the formula—reciting.

Preparation for review, the third *R*, can be made while reciting. A few key words can be put in outline form. When all sections are finished, the key words, or more detailed notes if preferred, provide the material for review. If questions and answers are easily recalled, the assignment is finished.

This method, like all good study methods, can be adapted to your needs. It can make your study more interesting, because finding answers to one's own questions takes the aimlessness out of reading. It can improve your ability to judge important items in the assignment. It can increase your power of concentration, because it makes you go to the heart of the matter to choose—and that is concentration. It will save much time, perhaps by increasing your speed of reading. In any case you will save time formerly spent wondering what you should look for as you studied. It can take the surprise and foreign element out of quizzes and tests, for you will have already asked yourself most of the questions. Like all good study habits, however, this formula will bring forth none of these desired results without conscious effort and prolonged practice.

No two people move exactly the same way in either bowling or brushing their teeth. No single set of study methods can be recommended for all. You must adapt to your needs those which seem to work best for you. All study methods are basically variations on the two that we have explained in detail.

One method which has received some attention is called simply the question method. However, the means for success encompass all the familiar ingredients of good study habits—survey, intensive reading, reciting, reviewing, etc.

Several years ago, Dr. Thomas F. Staton, of the Maxwell Air Force Base, prepared for Air Force officers a system designated as the *PQRST* method—preview, question, read, state, and test. Here again the essential factors are those which we have discussed.

Consider a sentence from Dr. Staton's preface in which he explains how his book, *How to Study*, came to be written: "When a number of them [Air Force officers] requesting help were asked if they had forgotten how to study, almost every one replied, 'No—I never learned.' "[2]

You can learn how to study while you are still young and your habits are more easily changed or formed. Adopt the methods of study best suited to you as an individual. Follow these suggestions to increase the effectiveness of the methods you choose.

Making good study methods work

1. Expect new study methods to produce results. You must be convinced that better habits will (1) help you find what you are expected to learn, (2) understand it more rapidly, (3) fix it in your mind more easily, and (4) improve your recitation and grades. Once convinced, discipline yourself against the hazards to learning. These are generally desperate, last-minute attempts which only confuse

[2]Thomas F. Staton, *How to Study* (McQuiddy Co., 1954).

you. One that causes many muddled and incorrect answers is cramming at the beginning of class, even while the teacher is making an announcement or assignment. Such an act shows either lack of preparation or lack of confidence. The impression made upon the teacher is one of indifference to good habits of study and poor planning.

2. Use whatever tactics are necessary to keep all study periods active. Inaction is learning's worst enemy. The long, grueling marathon is not study—avoid it. Several short periods, during which a keen sense of proper methods is kept in the front of the mind, are much better than a period that is lengthened into boredom. Experiments show that 25% higher grades are made by those who study material a half hour each day for five days than by those who spend one session of two-and-one-half hours. Remember this for pre-assigned tests and examinations.
3. All good study habits require an alertness for the effective use of textbook clues and built-in aids. Learn to watch for clues which lead into the "larger meaning" as opposed to those which introduce enumerated material. Use introductory paragraphs, summary paragraphs, and topic and summary sentences. Pay close attention to boldface and italic type, and all numbered items. Writers of manuals during World War II found that soldiers could learn material more easily if it were arranged in short paragraphs and numbered one, two, three, etc. Textbooks are not written to be read as one reads a novel. They are organized to present a specific amount of material in a defi-

nite way. An alertness of how the material is presented aids in the discovery of study clues. Special attention should be paid to illustrations, diagrams, maps, and charts. Much of the most significant material of the text is often given this graphic treatment.

4. Do not let details ruin your vision and perspective. Although you may handle small portions in study, avoid getting lost in detail. The first question, and one whose importance cannot be overlooked, is: "What am I supposed to learn from this assignment?" Failure to recognize *the larger meaning and patterns of relationship* leads to a condition not unlike trying to hold a dozen eggs in each hand without a basket. Package your details so that you can manage them. Do not miss the forest because you are looking only at the trees. A simple classroom experiment, conducted with two groups of students at Kent School, illustrates the tendency of the student to miss the forest. Each group was given a list of thirty items to be identified from a history assignment. The items were equally distributed to pertain to the life and work of three important historical characters in the assignment. To one group the teacher said, "These identifications can also be used to write detailed paragraphs on the life and work of Aristides, Themistocles, and Cimon." To the other group no such announcement was made. A test asking for a detailed paragraph on each man was given to both groups. The fifteen students who had been told how to put the trees together to see the forest averaged 82. The average of the fifteen who had been given the de-

tails only as identifications was 68. When the test was repeated, without further study, and the same material was asked for as simple identifications, the average of the same group was 80. This proved that although the group had sufficient information from the beginning, they lacked the vision to see it in a different light.

5. Use your common sense to judge which study methods are best for you. Only you can evaluate whether or not your preparation is easier and your recitation more thorough by using questions before or after reading. Only you can judge whether you need to write "working notes" for your review or whether you can handle it orally. Conscientious practice with different methods is the only honest means of arriving at a sound judgment.
6. Do not assume that good study methods are quite simple and not markedly different from your old reading and guessing methods. Directions for bowling, playing tennis, swimming, driving an automobile, and playing a guitar all sound quite simple when read. But learning any new skill requires much adaptation and practice. If you learn to use effective study methods you will have substituted new habits for old, and practiced equally as seriously as you have to achieve other skills. If you are willing to devote the time to it, the skill of study will prove far more important than all your other skills combined, for directly and indirectly it will make a contribution to all of them.

CHAPTER 6

Summaries and Outlines: Using Them and Learning from Them

Reducing quantity to quality

The words *summary* and *outline* conjure up the picture of the concentrated chocolate bar called "Chunky," into which has been packed flavor, energy, and hunger satisfaction of such quality that quantity is unnecessary. Both the summary and the outline reduce quantity to a refined quality of small dimension which aids understanding and memory. Both help the learner to picture the basic meaning and structure of what he is studying. Both aim at compactness and clarity.

There are great storehouses of summaries and outlines available to help you learn, and you will, of course, make many of your own during your school years and in whatever area you choose for your life's work. First, we will look at those which "like acres of diamonds in your own back-yard" are all around you, waiting to make your learning easier and provide you with models for your own summaries and outlines.

Finding models of condensations

Woodrow Wilson, who was a great educator as well as a great statesman, defined education as "Knowing where to find what you want." Try this simple experiment. If there is an encyclopedia or reference book at home, look up something that interests you—rockets, birds, horses, baseball, American Indians, or the island of Tasmania. Study the compactness, the choice and arrangement of details, and the fundamental image produced. You will be amazed at the completeness of the article. If you do not have an encyclopedia at home, use one in your school library or a public library.

Start with a junior encyclopedia, such as *World Book*, *Junior Britannica*, or any one that is available. Read the summarization of the history of your state or city. Read several biographies. Note carefully the division of topics, the choice of words, and the use of graphic material in dealing with population, industry, resources, etc. If there are one-volume encyclopedias on the reference shelf, compare the facts it presents with those of the multivolume works.

Equally as valuable as seeing how material is summarized is to learn what summaries already exist to help you. Are you enjoying your algebra class? Is the study of chemistry proving difficult for you? Are you confused about "Jacksonian Democracy" as it is presented in your textbook? Look up *algebra* in the encyclopedia. Here you will find the course, its principal parts, the methods of solving equations, and illustrations to clarify difficult problems. From a four-page summary your whole conception of the course may be changed. You may really understand for the first time what algebra is all about. Do the same for chemistry. The enlightenment resulting from such brief inquiry can change your attitude, your understanding, and your grades. Check "Jacksonian Democracy" first in a junior encyclopedia, then in a larger one or an encyclopedia of history. It is so easy to learn if you give a little thought to finding what you want.

Perhaps you have more than once been in a situation similar to the student reading Homer's *Iliad* in poetry translation who found that he could not follow the thread of the story. After much persuasion he looked up the *Iliad* in an encyclopedia. There he found it summarized by books. Book II, which was causing him so much trouble, was summarized in nine lines. The entire twenty-four books, with the thread of the story plainly given, was summarized in three-and-a-half pages. From this time on the student did not have to be persuaded to use the summaries available to him. He was able to read the *Iliad* and enjoy it. He discovered that the reference shelf in the library was filled with study aids which could clarify and save time.

Books of facts, general encyclopedias, and encyclopedias of specific subjects (history, literature, science), all contain summarized material that can provide quick clarification. Atlases, handbooks, and dictionaries of all kinds beckon from the reference shelf in the library. The use of carbon-14 to explain that Cro-

Magnon man's campfire in a cave in France burned 11,000 years ago sounds complicated and difficult. Look it up in a reference book. The whole process is summarized in half a column.

Weekly news magazines and book reviews often provide excellent examples of summarizing. The tables of contents of books, single-page condensations of school subjects, and pamphlet outline series can all be used to better your understanding of how you can make your own outline. We now turn to how you can summarize and outline with the skill of an encyclopedist.

The making of a good summary

A summary gives in condensed form the main points of a body of material. The points may be presented in the order of the original text, but this is not a requirement. However, a good summary does demand strict adherence to the following: (1) that no fundamental ideas be omitted; (2) that no new ideas be introduced; (3) that no general or editorial elements be attached to main ideas; (4) that the point of view of the original text be maintained; (5) that the summary be put in the writer's own vocabulary and not that of the original text.

The précis (French meaning precise and pronounced pray-see) is another form of condensing. In addition to the five requirements of a summary, the précis includes a sixth requirement suggested by its name. It follows precisely the order and proportion of the original text, and undertakes to maintain the original tone without requiring the vocabulary of the text.

You will also encounter the word "synopsis" (Greek *syn*—together and *opsis*—to see) in reference to summaries of stories or poems. A synopsis is a brief and general summary which provides a much broader picture than either a summary or a précis.

The ability to write a good summary will provide you with these advantages: (1) one of the best study methods for reviewing your work; (2) an improved ability to think and condense; (3) an aid to recalling the essentials of your work; (4) the skill to judge quickly between main points and contributing items; (5) the ability to organize and write smoother, more unified, and more complete answers on tests and examinations. This last advantage is perhaps the most valuable.

Most summary writing during your school years will be done either to review for or to answer questions. Some students mistakenly practice putting down a group of unrelated sentences and expect them to be accepted as a summary. They do not make a summary. An acceptable summary is a miniature composition. It begins with a topic sentence. It contains unity, coherence, and emphasis, as do all good compositions. Connection between sentences is indicated; if the summary is more than a single paragraph, proper transition is shown.

The inability to write a good summary is reflected in the complaints often heard immediately after tests. "I just couldn't write the answer. I knew it, but when I started to write I couldn't find the right words." Or haven't you heard some friend say, "I started with the first idea I thought of and then forgot to go back and put in the ones from the first part of the assignment."

It seems doubly tragic that a person knows the answer and yet fails to follow a line of thought which would give the teacher the "gist" of the material, organized and complete. This error can be corrected by knowing and using the methods of good summary writing.

Summary writing starts as a challenge. Reducing sentences to phrases, and phrases to meaningful words requires practice and the study of summary material provided by reference books. But economy of words can become an important part of your learning, a time saver that can also help improve your marks. The length of a summary will vary according to purpose and the requirements of your teachers. However, try to make your own review summaries less than one third the length of the original text. If after extensive practice you can reduce them to one fifth, it is even better. A well-written summary is a test of how completely you have understood a paragraph, a chapter, an assignment, or a book—and how concisely and clearly you have been able to condense it without losing its meaning.

The art of outlining

Outlining, like summary writing and note-taking, is a learning skill which aids clear thinking, good organization, and the ability to recall more easily what has been learned. The outline is a plan—a blueprint of ideas—and not many solid structures have been built satisfactorily without a plan. The outline does two important things with ideas: (1) It shows the order in which they are arranged. (2) It shows the relative importance of the individual ideas.

The correct outline form is accepted as standard

and cannot be varied. The form follows five specific rules: (1) A title is placed at the beginning, but is not numbered or lettered as part of the outline. (2) Roman numerals, used to designate main topics, are written to the left of the red margin on lined notebook paper or one inch in from the edge of unlined paper. (3) Subtopics are designated in descending order by capital letters, Arabic numerals, small letters, Arabic numerals in parentheses, and small letters in parentheses. (4) All subtopics are indented to the right; subtopics of equal rank are put directly under one another; those in each descending rank are placed under the first letter of the first word above them. (5) There are always two or more subtopics because subtopics are divisions of the topic above them.

Correct Outline Form

```
I.
    A.
    B.
        1.
        2.
            a.
            b.
                (1)
                (2)
                    (a)
                    (b)
II.
```

Incorrect Outline Form

```
I.
    A.
        1.
```

It is easily observed that no division has been made

in this incorrect form. *A* is the same as *I*, and *I* is the same as *A* and *I*. Until the topic is divided into subtopics it remains under *I*.

The outline may be of words, phrases, or sentences, depending upon the nature of the material and the purposes of the outline.

Word Outline

Sentences

I. Forms
   A. Simple
   B. Complex
   C. Compound
II. Kinds
   A. Declarative
   B. Interrogative
   C. Imperative
   D. Exclamatory

Topical (phrase) Outline

Steps in Writing a Theme

I. Planning the theme
   A. Choosing a topic
   B. Limiting the topic
   C. Making an outline
II. Writing the contents
   A. Making a first copy
   B. Correcting and revising
   C. Copying in final form

Sentence Outline

How to Improve Written Work

I. Daily papers can be improved by neatness and careful checking.
   A. Write each paper as neatly as you would like it if you had to mark it.

   B. Check for careless mistakes before the paper is handed in.
   C. Go over the paper when it is returned to check against repeating mistakes.

II. Weekly themes can be improved and made more readable through planning and interest.
   A. Choose a topic that can be limited to specifics rather than generalizations.
   B. Write with the expressed purpose of holding the reader's attention from the beginning of the first sentence to the end of the last.

III. Research themes can be improved by more and better organized information.
   A. Gather twice as much material as needed, and then use only that which touches directly upon the topic.
   B. Arrange all information logically before attempting an outline.
   C. Select and rearrange information that will provide balanced and proportionate content.

Outlines usually fall into one of several reasonable orders. Items may be arranged logically in (1) Time (chronological) order—such as biography or sequence of events. (2) Numerical order—according to size or number. An outline of coal-producing states would probably start with the one producing the most and go to the least or vice versa. (3) Alphabetical order—a rather arbitrary order used for convenience. For example, coal-producing states could be outlined alphabetically. (4) Place order—according to location. If one wished to emphasize the regional distribution of coal-producing states, place order could be used.

The key word is *logically*, as it pertains to the purpose of the outline. Our examples of word, phrase, and sentence outlines are arranged in time order, the logical sequence of events. In the outline of words it seems logical that sentence forms came before sentence kinds. Doubtless the first sentence to evolve was simple. The four kinds of sentences are arranged according to probable use; the declarative is perhaps the most used and the others follow in the order listed. The arrangement of ideas is a personal matter. The important thing is to have a logical reason for the arrangement.

Your use of outlining for study and review will usually mean no more than the condensation of textbook material. This will not be difficult because most textbooks are arranged in logical patterns of sequence and relationship. As in the case of summaries, encyclopedias, especially junior ones, provide excellent models of outlining. Many good outlines conclude articles that cover two or three pages. These encyclopedias and your English book should afford sufficient examples to help you become expert. Your greatest problem at first will be to reduce your outline to sensible proportions. There is always an inclination to include too much.

The outlining that will stretch your mind, and be most troublesome at the beginning, is that used for your original work—such as the outline of a theme or an essay examination question. Until you have developed the ability to blueprint your ideas mentally, it will probably be best to use the sentence-type outline for your themes. Putting the outline in sentence form seems to aid the beginner in establishing a better relationship between ideas.

Successful outlining is far more than following a mechanical form to sort out and arrange ideas. It is a creative exercise, practiced all the time, because whenever we plan we are outlining. In reality, it is the skill whereby we put things (ideas, furniture, or flowers) in their proper place and perspective. Outlining is one of the important learning processes in the development of clear thinking.

Individual methods of condensing

Specific advantages can also be found in condensation methods other than the standard summary and outline. Working notes for review and recall may take several forms. Some students use summary texts. A summary text is a one-sentence statement of a section, chapter, or assignment, recorded daily to give a bird's-eye view of the course at test time. Recitation keys are also useful. They are usually words or phrases written in parallel columns. Sometimes they compare and contrast.

Example:

Mississippi	*Amazon*
Length:	Length:
Flood season:	Flood season:
Navigation:	Navigation:

Sometimes they merely classify.

Example:

Great Historians	*Great Dramatists*
Herodotus	Aeschylus
Thucydides	Sophocles
Polybius	Euripides

One excellent pattern of recitation key is the multiple column:

Who?	*When?*	*What?*
Darwin	1850	Origin of the Species

Ingenious and helpful methods of condensing can be developed by each student to satisfy both need and subject. However, these methods will not replace effective summary writing and outlining. All have a purpose and are invaluable to the student who wants to *remember more, review it in less time, and write it more intelligently on tests.*

Suggestions for better summary writing

1. Read and study with summary intent. Condition your mind to summarize. Practice summarizing with pleasure reading—newspapers, magazines, and novels. As you study textbooks and other work-type reading, visualize the pattern of unity you would use for a summary answer.
2. Train yourself to replace the author's words with your own, but don't settle for just an equivalent word. Try to select an equally impressive or a better synonym. This makes your summary so personal that recall is almost automatic.
3. Practice economy of words. Link parallel details together. Use semicolons to emphasize in one sentence what is expressed in the original text in three. Learn to link ideas in series for easy recall. Practicing economy of words is an aid in separating main points from nonessential introductory and illustrative material.
4. Avoid generalization, unnecessary lead-ins, and double conclusions. Learn to distinguish between opinion and fact. If you are writing about Washington at Valley Forge, it is probably unwise to start by reminding your teacher that Washington was the commander in chief of the Continental

Army. You need not repeat, in a last dangling sentence, the fact that Washington had a trying winter at Valley Forge; that's what you have just finished summarizing.

5. Learn to distinguish between fragmentation and summarization. Fragmentation is a haphazard recording of ideas from an assignment. A good summary is a miniature theme that contains the elements of unity, coherence, and emphasis.
6. Do not content yourself with reading one or two summaries and accepting them as models. Make comparisons between topics you are studying and encyclopedia articles on these topics. The reference shelf in a library is a storehouse of models.

Suggestions for better outlines

1. Observe carefully the standard outline form. Any change, transposition, or incorrect indentation is evidence of disregard for order and accepted authority.
2. Avoid the most common error in outlining—leaving off the title or designating it as a main topic.
3. Be sure your outline performs two functions: (1) the arrangement of ideas; and (2) the relative importance of the ideas.
4. Remember that a subtopic results from division of a topic. Therefore, there will always be at least two subtopics—*A.* and *B.*, *1.* and *2.*, *a.* and *b.* Nothing that is divided can remain whole (one); it will become two, three, etc., depending upon the number of separate parts.
5. Know the orders of outlines: (1) time, (2) numerical, (3) alphabetical, and (4) place. With each

use the key word *logical* to give ideas the most sensible arrangement. If you can reasonably explain your arrangement, your outline is probably in good order.

6. Use the outline as an aid to memory, a blueprint for easy recall, an organizational frame for written tests and themes, and a time-saver at examination time. The only students who get their money's worth from textbooks are those who develop outlining into a regular and efficient study skill.
7. Perhaps a review of note-taking in Chapter 2 might be helpful at this time.

CHAPTER 7

Words: How to Improve Your Knowledge of Them

The many qualities of words

Words are the tools of thinking. Beginning with the grunts and ejaculations of our remote ancestors, words have flowered into their many uses, written and otherwise, to provide man with a history totally different from the lower primates. Who could underestimate the important part that words have played in making this difference?

The purpose of this word study is to help you increase your vocabulary, adapt it to more meaningful use, and raise your grades. If there seems to be delay in offering suggestions for dictionary use, keeping lists of new words, and putting new words to work, do not be impatient. These are back-door methods necessary for those who somehow miss the excitement of entering word study by the front door, and the front door of word study is interest.

The origin of words

"Etymology is the study of," says your dictionary, "the origin and development of a word; tracing a word as far back as possible." The word etymology comes from two Greek words—*etymon*, meaning "true sense," and *ology*, meaning "the study of." Etymology usually uses the method of linguistic comparisons, an exciting means of discovering the romance behind our everyday language. Add to this the origin of dozens of names around you, and word study takes on an absorbing and fascinating quality found in few subjects.

Think briefly of several names around you. There is a mountain named Hawk's Peak, another named Candlewood. Long ago the Indians watched hawks soar above the peak, brushing the sky with their wings, and named the mountain. The frontiersman, having gone to gather pitch pine to light his frontier cabin and substituting the pine torch for candles, named the mountain where he found the candle wood—Candlewood Mountain. Etymology, begun with the familiar which lies before your very eyes, and extended to your dictionary, will not only enrich your vocabulary, it will also make you word conscious and indirectly improve your ability to read with more comprehension and spell more correctly.

To attempt an imaginative picture of the origin of a single word is to journey into a remote past of mere conjecture. The evolution of words reaches so far back in time, perhaps 80,000 years, that beginnings can only be surmised. It taxes the imagination to think how many thousands of years signs and grunts were used before words came into existence. About 4000 years ago man advanced his evolution of speech and words into a new epoch; he began to write. First he scratched strangely and crudely on stone, or perhaps used a pointed stick in the sand. Later he progressed to bits of hardened clay; finally his materials included papyrus, parchment, and paper. How did he begin? Probably he began with a picture. Slowly the picture came to represent an idea. The idea came to be represented by a symbol—a symbol that could be read and uttered. This was a word.

How particular sounds came to represent particular things is also part of the fascinating story of words. In Plato's shortest dialogue, *Cratylus*, covering only four pages, Socrates speculates on the origin of words. He suggests that many names indicate the nature of the thing named; some names express rest while others show motion. The sound of *l* seems to suggest the *lull* that *lures* toward the *lunar* world of rest. How many words with *l* can you list?—leisure, lullaby, lassitude, lazy—the lengthening *list* makes one *listless*. On the other hand, the sound of *r* suggests motion—run, race, rowdy, rodeo, rattle, ruin, ripple. Ripple suggests that some words echo the sound of the thing for which they stand. (The ripples crept quietly under the overhanging bank. The brook babbled its protest to the rocks as it raced along.)

There have been many theories regarding word origins and names since the time of Socrates. Was the Indian who looked out from his campsite high on the Blue Ridge Mountains naming the beautiful valley below? Was he echoing the caress of earth and sky at the edge of the vast panorama? Or was he raising his arms in awesome devotion to the daughter-of-the-skies? Anyway, the word he made was Shen-an-doah,

Shenandoah. Is there a single valley more beautifully named? And what of Je-ru-sa-lem—that beautiful, musical word? How came the word—from David's harp or the wind whispering among the promontory rocks?

The excitement of words

We must now turn to the practical, and deal with dictionaries and other aids which will increase your vocabulary. A thousand word games, histories, and stories are all about you daily. Do not let the fascination of words be clouded or lost. Every word was in its beginning a stroke of genius. According to Emerson, "Every word was once a poem." "Uttering a word," said Ludwig Wittgenstein, "is like striking a note on the keyboard of the imagination."

By a magical stroke of genius one word became a sound to call unseen beauty to mind. It made possible the conveyance of an idea or impression from one man to another. Seeing was no longer necessary in order to understand. Slowly, words acquired new uses and distinctions so that they could picture feelings, circumstances, and abstractions. As time passed, at first awkward but later improved combinations of words made clearer pictures. Time found at last some remote ancestor of ours who with excitement began to put words in rhythmic forms and create beauty. Thus poetry was born, which is, said Samuel Coleridge, "the best words in the best order."

But the putting together of words to produce distinctive and understandable prose demands that combinations be used to deal quietly and justly with the common feelings of people, and to give beauty and loftiness to things of the everyday world. If not lifted up these feelings are sometimes lost in the drab words of grocery lists, little complaints in little language, and repetitions stamped with dullness.

Ways to improve your vocabulary

How can you put your love of words into action—"to write well and to speak well"? The first step is to make friends with a book that will prove your lifelong companion—the dictionary. How many people have ever bothered to look up the origin and meaning of the word "dictionary"? It comes from the Latin word *dictio*, meaning *to speak, to point out in words.* The dictionary speaks to us about words. It tells us: (1) from whence they came; (2) how to pronounce them; (3) what parts of speech they are; (4) how to spell them; (5) their meanings; (6) words which mean the same—called synonyms; and (7) antonyms—words that have opposite meanings.

Here the fascination of word study leads to discovery. Synonym and antonym—there is something about each which is the same. *Onym* appears in both words. *Sŷn* and *ant* give the two words their opposite meanings. Both are prefixes, word parts attached to the front of a word to change its meaning. The foundation word to which the prefix is attached is called the root. Almost half of the more than 600,000 words in our language come from about 800 root words. So one way to build your vocabulary is to become keenly aware of root words. Besides the prefix and the root, there is a third word part called the suffix. The suffix is added to the end of a word to change its meaning. More will be said concerning the three word parts; for the moment let us return to synonym and antonym.

Syn is a prefix meaning *with, together with,* and *in time with. Onym* is from the Greek word *onoma* meaning *name*. Thus *synonym* means *with the same name*; simply translated it signifies *the same* meaning. What ideas now form around words such as synod, syndicate, synthesis, syndrome? Look up *syn* in your dictionary, and then check the roots of some of the words beginning with *syn. Ant* (anti) is a prefix meaning *against*, so *antonym* would mean *against the name*, therefore, opposing or opposite. How many words can you think of whose meanings are much clearer since you know what the suffix means? What about antipathy, antacid, antagonist? Look up the derivations of prefix and suffix. Only by continued use will you be able to make your dictionary an exciting game book and, at the same time, one of your most useful tools of learning.

Using the dictionary

Here are some things you should know about using your dictionary: (1) The two words printed at the top of the page are the first and last words defined on the page. Noting these at a glance can save you time spent looking for a word that is not on the page. (2) The word is divided into syllables; usually a (·) separates the syllables. (3) The pronunciation is indicated by accent marks and the sound spelling of the word. For example, documentary (dok′yoo men′ta ri). All accent marks are explained in one of the beginning sections of the dictionary. These sections and other introductory material should be reviewed. (4) The letters in boldface type, for example, **n., v., adj., adv.,** show the part of speech—noun, verb, adjective, or adverb. (5) The derivation, (G) Greek, (L) Latin, (AS) Anglo-Saxon, etc., indicates the language from which the word has come down to us. (6) The definitions are next; the most common uses are given first. (7) Most dictionaries conclude with one or more synonyms. Some also give antonyms.

Few people avail themselves of the complete program for word study offered by the dictionary. Many use it only to check spelling. Some use it hurriedly for word meaning, usually reading only the first definition. Those who appreciate words, strive to master their use, and add beauty and understanding to their speech and writing measure carefully both meaning and synonym for the most effective use. Only when used in this manner can the dictionary provide an avenue of improvement.

The dictionary habit can be made doubly successful if accompanied by a degree of honest admission—that many of the words used daily are known by sight, but are really not known precisely enough to be useful as a tool of learning. Day after day, many students pass over words in each of their subjects which they would never think of looking up in the dictionary. They are sure they know the meaning. But do they know *the meaning* that would make the word into a real tool of thinking as it pertains to the subject being studied?

Here are some words chosen from ninth-grade English, history, and mathematics textbooks. Do you know the exact meaning of each as it relates to the particular subject?

English	*History*	*Mathematics*
mediocre	medieval	median
concentrate	convocation	congruent
manifold	manifest	manipulate
monograph	monopoly	monomial
theme	theory	theorem
analysis	analyze	dialyze
dialectic	diadem	diagonal
quotation	quorum	quotient
conjunction	community	complement
modify	mobilization	measure
declarative	declaration	denominator
predicate	repudiate	assimilate
relative	radical	radical
phrase	faction	fraction

Understanding meaning as it applies to English, history, or mathematics can make your work easier to understand. Look up several of the familiar words listed above and see whether or not you have been using them in the way that clarifies the subject matter. This is the second step in increasing your vocabulary and your grades—learning to be aware of words you see and use every day, but really have not used to their fullest value.

Word study through word parts

Conscientious study of the three word parts—prefix, root, and suffix—is the third step toward vocabulary improvement and the generation of an insatiable appetite for new words. We have already mentioned the fact that almost half the 600,000 words in our language are derived from about 800 root words. Two Greek words, *grapho* (to write) and *logos* (word, speech, knowledge, thought) are the roots of more than 400 words. Beginning with telegraph and philology (*phil-sin*, love—*logos*, word) see how many words you can write without using your dictionary. When you have twelve from each root you may turn to the dictionary for help.

Many words are formed by combinations of roots. The word *telegram* is made from the Greek word, *tele*, meaning *far off*, and the Greek word *gram*, meaning *letter*. From the Latin word *ped*, meaning *foot*, come pedal, pedometer, pedestal, pedestrian, and strangely enough, even pedigree. Look up pedigree in your dictionary. How many words can you build on the Latin root *porto*, to carry?

The word *root* is well chosen, for as the root of a tree supplies its means of growth, so does a large and vigorous vocabulary grow from an acquaintance with root words. Not only do meanings and new words emerge without the constant use of the dictionary, but spelling becomes much easier. S. Stephenson Smith lists ten Latin roots from which more than 2000 of our words come:[1]

capio	take, seize	plico	fold
duco	lead	pono	place
facio	do, make	tendo	stretch
fero	bear, carry	teneo	hold, have
mitto	send	specio	observe, see

As a beginning, try to find two words that come from each of the ten roots. Now try these last root games. The Latin word for hands is *manes*. See how many words you can write that come from this root. Start with *manuscript*. The Greek word *holos* means *whole*.

[1]S. Stephenson Smith, *The Command of Words* (New York: Thomas Y. Crowell Co., 1935).

Can you guess the meaning of holograph and holocaust?

A knowledge of roots plus the ability to recognize prefixes and suffixes will open up a whole new vocabulary world if you are willing to take apart and rebuild all the unfamiliar words you encounter. Here are some of the most frequently used prefixes and suffixes, and their meanings. Perhaps it is not necessary to memorize the entire list, but you should use it for handy reference until it is a part of your working vocabulary.

Prefix	*Meaning*	*Example*
a, ab	from, away	avert, abstain
a, an	without	atheist, anarchist
ad, af, at	to	adhere, affix, attain
ambi	both	ambidextrous
amphi	around	amphitheater
ant, anti	against	antonym, antipathy
ante	before	antedate
cata	down	cataract, catacomb
con, cor	with, together	convene, correlate
contra	against	contradict
de	from, down	descend, debase
di	apart	divert, divorce
dia	through	diameter, diagonal
dis	not	disagree, disappear
e, ex	out of, over	elude, export
em	out	emanate
em	in	embark
en	in	enclose
hyper	above, over	hypercritical
hypo	under	hypodermic
il	not	illegal, illegible
im	in, not	import, impossible
in	not	inactive
ir	not	irresponsible
per	through	permeate
peri	around	perimeter
post	after	postpone, posterity
pre	before	predict, precede

pro	for, forth	pronoun, procession
re	back, again, down	recall, revive, retreat
sub	under	subordinate
super	over, above	supervise
trans	across	transport, transmit

Suffixes, which are attached to the end of a word, usually change the part of speech—create, creat*ion*—or the degree of modification—hope*ful*, hope*less*. You should have a working knowledge of the basic list of suffixes which follows.

Suffix	*Meaning*	*Example*
able, ible	may be, capable of	digestible, reliable
ac, acy, al, ial	pertaining to	cardiac, legacy, national, facial
ance, ence	state of being	abundance, obedience
ant, ent, er, or, ive	verb to noun	servant, student, teacher, sailor, executive
ful, ous	full of	hopeful, joyous
ish, ity	the quality of	mannish, humility
less	without	voiceless, sleepless
ly	like	manly, cheerfully
ness, ry	state of	goodness, rivalry

Suffixes are too numerous to list exhaustively. They are the word parts which change the nature of words—nouns into adjectives, degrees of modification, adjectives into adverbs, verbs into nouns, and vice versa. The basic list will make it easy for you to recognize hood (man*hood*), ship (author*ship*), ize (central*ize*), some (whole*some*), ment (treat*ment*), and the many more which cannot be listed here.

Putting new words to work

The fourth and final step for vocabulary improvement is the use of new word lists or, far better and much more adaptable to study, new word cards. You may keep a list of new words and their meanings in your notebook, especially a list of basic vocabulary words which apply to a particular subject, such as biology, chemistry, history, or geometry. The word should be written with the definition that is directed toward the subject. If there are synonyms which help fix the word's meaning in your mind, they should be written in a column to the right of the definition as shown:

New Word *Definition* *Synonym*

However, the card system for new words is highly recommended. Most students find it more workable and adaptable. Vocabulary builder cards which can be bought are highly advisable for vocabulary study of a foreign language; but for your English vocabulary, a great deal of enjoyment can come from building your own. Buy the smallest index cards you can find. Keep them handy as you read or study. When you come upon a new word, write it on the front of the card. On the back write the definition or definitions and a synonym or two. Carry half a dozen or more cards with you or display them on your desk until you have put them in your working vocabulary; that is, until you are using them in conversation and in writing. This will seldom take more than three or four days. The cards may then be filed alphabetically or by subject vocabulary. Just a few weeks of practice and the new word cards become second nature. They can be studied while riding or walking to and from classes, waiting for a bus, and at numerous other odd moments. Put the new word card system to work to improve your vocabulary and your grades.

Summary of practices for vocabulary improvement

1. Use your dictionary. When you come upon a new word, a new use for an old word, or a word which you think you know but are not sure of, reach for your dictionary. Always keep it within easy reach. Some of your more technical textbooks may have a glossary at the front or the back. The glossary provides the meanings of technical words pertaining to the particular subject and may also supply meanings for new scientific words—so new that they are not in your dictionary. Technical words, explanatory concepts, definitions, and rules of special meaning may be conveniently arranged in the front or the back of your algebra, biology, chemistry, literature, or history textbook. Your dictionary study may lead you to other helpful books: *A Dictionary of Modern English Usage*, H. W. Fowler; Fernald's *Synonyms and Antonyms*; and Roget's *Thesaurus of English Words and Phrases*. The word *thesaurus* comes from the Latin word meaning treasure. Indeed, all dictionaries are treasures; the last named may be purchased in economically priced paperbacks. Why not add a treasure or two to your study desk?
2. Avoid word blindness. Although you use some words daily, you are not certain of their meaning. Some words which you read as part of assignments would add much to your understanding of the subject if you really knew them. Try these methods for teaching yourself to become aware of familiar words which are really strangers to you: (1) Begin

seeing the word whenever you come upon it. Study how it is used by others. (2) Question your own use in comparison to the uses of others. (3) Use your dictionary to find out if you are getting the most out of the familiar word. (4) Apply a specific meaning that will make your algebra, geometry, or social studies easier for you to understand. Vagueness is the curse attending many of the words we use without really knowing their meaning.

3. Become a word surgeon. Learn to dissect words into their parts—prefix, root, and suffix. Study word parts until a glance reveals the pattern of the word —whether it is a single root or built upon prefix, root, suffix, two roots, or some other combinations. Divide autobiography, bibliography, pandemonium, and transmutation into word parts. A working knowledge of a few fundamental parts, keen powers of observation, and conscientious practice is the fast way to add new words to your vocabulary.
4. Put new words to work. Ensure a working knowledge by recording each new word along with its definition and synonym. A sentence of your own, using the word, is also helpful. New word lists and new word cards are recommended ways of keeping records. A word is part of your working vocabulary when you can *pronounce it*, *spell it*, and *use* it in both conversation and writing. New words will not remain alive unless they are allowed to work.
5. Use the unlimited and fascinating word-world that surrounds you. John Ruskin defined genius as "a superior power of seeing." Why not use this definition to give yourself the quality of genius in word

study? Exercise that "superior power of seeing" to enjoy place names, your own names, words derived from people's names, trade names, words that name our foods, our days, our weeks, our months, and our seasons. Make a game of improving your vocabulary and your ability to use that vocabulary. "To carry the feelings of childhood into the powers of manhood," said Coleridge, "to combine the child's sense of wonder and novelty with the appearance which every day for years has rendered familiar, that is the character and privilege of genius. . . ." Keep "the child's sense of wonder and novelty" in your word study.

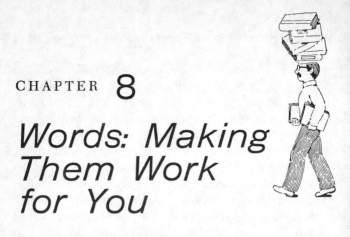

CHAPTER 8

Words: Making Them Work for You

The power of usage

"I don't know what you mean by 'glory,'" Alice said.

Humpty Dumpty smiled contemptuously, "Of course you don't—till I tell you. I meant 'there's a nice knock-down argument for you!'"

"But 'glory' doesn't mean 'a nice knock-down argument,'" Alice objected.

"When I use a word," Humpty Dumpty said in rather a scornful tone, "it means just what I choose it to mean—neither more nor less."

Lewis Carroll,
Through the Looking Glass

"Words are the tools of thinking," as we learned in Chapter 7. These fragile verbal tools, like all tools, may be kept keen-edged, polished, and productive, if used properly; they may become rusty, blunt-edged, and ineffective by careless, indifferent misuse and neglect. As distinctly shaped chisels are fashioned to carve a particular groove or pattern, so also the tools of thinking must be used with the concern of a master craftsman.

To use the tools of thinking most effectively, you must first ask yourself what qualities you wish to achieve through word use. Do pomposity, ostentation, pretentiousness, and ornamentation—fringed with garbled and garish vocabulary gingerbread—produce the word pictures that give meaning and understanding to our thoughts? Are not clarity, simplicity, sincerity, and orderliness—whose by-product is beauty—the things for which we aim? Is this not the pattern of all utterances which are our heritage and our models? Would you not agree that proper use of the tools of thinking comes "more from attitudes of mind than from principles of composition"?

On November 19, 1863, a national cemetery was dedicated at Gettysburg, Pennsylvania. Here, during the first three days of the previous July, thousands of soldiers had died. Senator Edward Everett was the principal speaker at the dedication. He dealt with the concepts of government, the evolution of democracy, and many other profound abstractions for an hour and fifty-five minutes. The world has forgotten what he said, but it remembers Lincoln's 287-word Gettysburg Address. Why? Because seldom in history have the tools of thinking been guided by "attitudes of the mind" to produce such clarity, simplicity, sincerity, and ordered beauty.

Requirements for effective use

As we turn to the uses to which words can be put, the attributes they take on, and how you can make them work best for you, bear in mind the four qualities which produce beauty: (1) clarity, (2) simplicity, (3) sincerity, and (4) orderliness. These must stand guard over whatever you speak or write; these must be the primary elements of your style; these must be the qualities which your teachers, your readers, and your listeners find as you express your thoughts.

Half amusingly, but perhaps with more truth than will ever be known, it has been said that if Winston Churchill, in his famous speech to the British people after he became prime minister in 1940, had used words such as "wounds, unrelenting labor, weeping, and perspiration," instead of the simple "blood, toil, tears, and sweat"—the British people might not have rallied to fight against Hitler.

The world knows no force sufficient to stand against the power of simple words. As the strength of a parachute is derived from each tiny thread, so is the strength of an idea dependent upon each fragile verbal tool. The strength and completeness of each recitation, each question you ask your teacher, each answer you write on tests and examinations, will depend upon how wisely you choose and use your words.

Viewpoint is an important consideration in choosing the words you use. They must be selected for the person or persons to whom you wish to convey your thoughts. When Abraham Lincoln spoke at Gettysburg, he did not choose words for himself and the dignitaries who were present. He selected words which had meaning for the veterans of the battle who leaned on their crutches or dangled empty uniform sleeves in the November wind. He knew that among his listeners were mothers who had lost sons, wives who had lost husbands, and brothers who had lost brothers. These people would remember what he said because he spoke for them.

Churchill, in his famous "Blood, Sweat, and Tears" speech, did not choose his words for the members of Parliament. He chose them for the thousands of Britishers who would bleed and sweat, and bleed and sweat some more, in the impending holocaust.

There are a number of questions you should ask yourself in order to capture the point of view of the person to whom you wish to communicate: (1) What words will he clearly understand? (2) What would he really like to hear? (3) What are his interests? (4) What are his needs? The last question is the most significant.

Once you have answered these questions, you must extend the point of view to respect the hearer's or reader's conception of his or her abilities. Most people consider themselves capable of observing and assessing human nature, as well as being capable of imagination, broadened vision, adapting to new ideas, and sympathetic understanding.

When you have convinced yourself that the listener's point of view, and not your own, is important, other judgments in word selection follow. The function of introductory words, key words, signal, transitional, and terminal words, and the best word to perform each function must be considered. These are all announcement words; they introduce an idea, they clarify and emphasize, they signal importance, change of thought, and conclusions; and many perform more than one function. Here are some of the most commonly used:

now
probably
of course
for instance
for example
although
consequently
finally
therefore
actually
because
however
distinctly
while
results
principles
comparison
influences

altogether
nevertheless
besides
moreover
furthermore
first
second
then
those
these
only
also
former
latter
significance
effects
contrast
implications

rather
finally
usually
next
always
all
few
none
some
never
initially
during
in addition
too
causes
innovations
essentials
facts

These are practical, everyday, working words. Some do little more than substitute for a period to separate thoughts, yet the person who desires to use words to the best advantage will not shrug them off as having no significance. Many of these words imply conditions which range from slight probability to unqualified certainty. These are words which we often ignore in our reading, and when we do, we get less from what we read.

In order to put more power into your use of this type of word, and to get more from it in your study, try the following: (1) Study the use of these functional words as you read your assignments. (2) Read from some of the great writers—Herodotus, Thucydides, Cicero, Ruskin, Thoreau, Emerson, Churchill, or Samuel E. Morison. Note with what care they use this type of word to clarify their message. (3) Listen for this type of word in the conversation of others and judge critically for effectiveness. This will guide you towards both self-evaluation and improvement.

Finally, always remember that the use of the word really determines its character. What is an everyday word in one person's vocabulary becomes beautiful as another uses it. Lincoln didn't say, "At this time we are engaged"; he said, "Now we are engaged," and *now* was something more than time; it was a part of each listener. He did not say, "It is *wholly*, or *completely* fitting"; he said, "It is *altogether* fitting," and the act became more than a good idea to which no one could object. It became "altogether fitting and proper"—a total necessity, involving all.

Many meanings and shades of meanings

To speak and write with clarity and simplicity you must know the different meanings and shades of meanings which many familiar words have. Most words have one or two denoted meanings; that is, explicit meanings. The same words may also have several implied or associated meanings, often called the connoted meanings.

Let's look at the words denote and connote. Both come from the Latin word *nota,* meaning *mark.* The prefix *de* means down; therefore, the denoted meaning is the *marked down* (definite, expressed) meaning. The prefix *con* means *with* or *together*; thus, connote may be defined as *gathered to the word.* Connoted meanings have become associated with a word.

Let's see how many meanings have become associated with the root word *mark* used above.

Use	*Meaning*
Denoted:	
To make a mark (verb)	Mark your notebook for easy identification.
A line, dot, etc. (noun)	Who put the mark on the desk?
Gonnoted:	
To wait	She will mark time until summer.
A sign or indication	The ability to listen is the mark of a civilized person.
To listen, heed	Mark my words, she will not return.
A sign of evil	He is cursed with the mark of Cain.
A standard of quality	This paper is not up to the mark.
Importance, distinction	The chairman is a man of mark.
Impression	She left her mark on her students.
A guide or point of reference	The harbor lights were a mark for fliers.
A target	He did not hit the mark.
An aim, goal	The mark of the campaign was to raise $6000.
A nautical term	Bits of leather indicated the marks on the sounding line. Samuel Clemens adopted the riverboat call "mark twain" as his pen name.
To show plainly	Her smile marked her happiness.
To be ready	I am on my mark.

See how many connoted meanings you can find for the following familiar words: term, take, tag, table, tack, sweep, snap, spread, train, and pick. The simple word *run* has more than a dozen connoted meanings. Write your own meaning for each use as shown in the sentences which follow:

1. The boys have the *run* of the club.
   Meaning:
2. The bus *runs* past Brentano's.
   Meaning:
3. The depression caused a *run* on the banks.
   Meaning:
4. She got a *run* in her stocking from kneeling.
   Meaning:
5. He *runs* the assembly with an iron hand.
   Meaning:
6. The deer *run* leads across the field to the pond.
   Meaning:
7. *Green Pastures* had one of the longest *runs* in theatrical history.
   Meaning:
8. Maris made another home *run*.
   Meaning:
9. The mayor had a close *run* in the election.
   Meaning:
10. The fishermen had a *run* of good luck on trout.
    Meaning:
11. The broker *runs* up a big telephone bill.
    Meaning:
12. Anton *ran* the spear through the door.
    Meaning:
13. Cleveland *ran* for president twice.
    Meaning:
14. Pasteur *ran* down the cause of the silkworms dying in Provençal.
    Meaning:

Distinctive use lifts the common and familiar out of

the realm of the ordinary. You can greatly improve your ability to handle words by replacing many overused and tired words with more pointed and graphic connotative ones. Read with a keen eye for finding new uses for the many words which previously had only one or two meanings for you.

You can make meanings clear by examining the use of the word in the sentence. A word may have meanings that are almost opposite, as shown by the uses of *fast* in this sentence: The torpedo was *fast* approaching its target; seconds before it had been *fast* in its tube. The first connotes great speed and the second implies a lack of motion. As with new words, you must put new meanings to work if you expect to keep them in your vocabulary.

One of the glorious achievements of man, said Sophocles, was that "he has learned the use of language to express windswift thought." (Agard translation.) Another translation puts it in slightly different words:

Words also, and thought as rapid as air,
He fashions to his good use.[1]

Which words impress us most when we hear or read them? Surely, those which produce action and bring a thought to life. Words which, as Sophocles puts it, express thoughts as swift as wind.

[1]Dudley Fitts, ed. and trans., *Greek Plays* (New York: The Dial Press, 1947).

The person who masters the use of words is always on the alert for the more active word—the one that will react upon the senses. What is it in a poem or story, a dialogue or speech, that makes us *see* the thing being described? When do we *hear* the sea splashing against the rocks? How do we *smell* the pleasant countryside or the ever-descending, constantly darkening smog of the noisy street? What gives *taste* to the banquet or picnic? When do we *feel* most keenly the sensation of holding a newborn lamb, the breath of April, the blast of January wind, or the loneliness of the accused in a stark, oak-paneled courtroom? All the questions have the same answer—when active words are used.

The most important characteristic of life is action, and speaking and writing which reflect the thoughts of life most effectively do so through action. For that reason it is always better to use the active rather than the passive voice of verbs. To say "Fishing is enjoyed by John," (passive voice) leaves John motionless; but to say "John enjoys fishing," (active voice) starts him on his way and makes him act upon something.

After the subject, which is the reason for the expression of the thought, the verb is *the important word*. It carries the weight, contains the vigor, and, if carefully chosen, is capable of sound and color. Note the verbs in the sentences which follow:

1. Greece *declined* rapidly after the Battle of Mantinea in 362 B.C.; both political and cultural strength were gone.
2. Greece was *doomed* after the Battle of Mantinea in 362 B.C.; decadence, debility, and despair prevailed.

Even though the verb *declined* is given a modifier to speed the action, it does not bring Greece crashing down with the resounding sense and sound of *doom.* And what of *were gone* as compared with *prevails*? The tense of *were gone* removes the action of political and cultural strength, but action remained–decadence, debility, and despair *prevailed.*

Selections and judgment concerning them

Although sound is useful, it must never be allowed to obscure meaning. Alliteration, the repetition of an initial sound as in *d*oomed, *d*ecadence, *d*ebility, *de*-spair, must be used cautiously. Will the reader get a clear picture from these words? Is it possible that the concreteness of *political* and *cultural strength* is desirable? These and many other questions will constantly confront you if your aim is clarity, simplicity, sincerity, and orderliness.

Diction, the name given to choice of words, demands a special concern for concreteness in words. As noted above, we might find alliteration pleasing to the ear. We might have many favorite abstract words –decadence, prosperity, patience, charity, temptation. But if solid nouns and verbs can create an exact word picture, naming the subject and action of decay, or of prosperity, or of patience, then pleasant generalizations and abstractions must be passed over for the sake of clarity. The use of concrete words makes the user a first-hand dealer; abstractions make him a second-hand dealer.

Careless selection and mental laziness cause vague and confusing abstractions. The stone mason would give little care to his choice of stones if he cared nothing about the pattern and the looks of his wall. The hardest part of building the wall is choosing the correct stone. Expressing your thoughts accurately is hard work, and finding the correct concrete word is the hardest part of all.

Generalization is soft, subject to misinterpretation, and sometimes popular, because it can be adapted to compromise. Concreteness is solid, precise, totally devoid of vagueness, and graphically natural. Your words will be judged forceful or weak, and this judgment will be based essentially on the concreteness of your words.

Concrete words need few modifiers. Try to avoid overworked adjectives. If you use an adjective at all, test it for efficiency: is it the right adjective or is there a brighter, better one? Make the same judgment of adverbs, for nothing can muddle a word picture as quickly as "excess baggage" adverbs. If the verb is strong, weigh the contribution of the adverb carefully before you add it. If the horse *galloped* over the pasture, it is unnecessary to add that it galloped *rapidly*. The adverb modifying the adjective must also be studied with a critical eye. If the adjective has already "put the icing on the cake," further icing or decoration might reflect only poor taste and contribute only to confusion. When modifiers are necessary, choose the most exact of several synonyms.

Summary of practices for word use improvement

1. Choose the words you use from the point of view of your listener or reader. Words are only labels that we use for easy identification; these labels

must mean the same to your listener or reader as they do to you. There is a story of a little girl who told her mother that the Sunday school teacher told the class he would drop them in the furnace if they were absent on three successive Sundays. The child, living in a house with an old-fashioned, gravity-flow, hot air furnace below a large register in the hallway, had confused the labels. The Sunday school teacher had actually said he would drop them from the *register*.

2. There is a "best" word for introducing, signalling, transmitting, and concluding. The best word gives the best directions. Here are some words and phrases to avoid:

   Due to–overworked and awkward. *Because* or *on account of* are much better.
   Inside of–do not use *of*. *Inside* is complete.
   Later on–do not use *on*. *Later* is complete.
   Off of–do not use *of*. *Off* is complete.
   Plan on–do not use *on*. *Plan* is complete.
   Rarely ever–do not use *ever*. *Rarely* is complete.
   Seldom ever–do not use *ever*. *Seldom* is complete.
   Subsequent to–awkward substitute for *after*. Use *after*.
   Transpire–used incorrectly as a substitute for *occurred*. Means to *become known*, not *to happen*.

3. Knowing and using the different meanings of many ordinary words is an effective way to add clarity and color to your thought pictures. Study connoted meanings which give finer shades of meaning and different degrees and aspects of the same thought. Replace the overworked "blanket" words used to create general pictures of ideas with fresher syn-

onyms. Count the number of times you use *went* when you could use walked, ran, tiptoed, stole, raced, or stumbled. Do not overuse such words as terrible, nice, good, bad, difficult, or splendid. Count the number of times you use *building* when you could use church, courthouse, bank, store, dwelling, or apartment house. Learn to choose the word that exactly pictures the idea.

4. Search for the active word and use it to give movement to your word pictures. Choose words which react on all the senses, not just sight. If you write, "She was happy," only vision is possible. If you write, "She laughed aloud," she is also heard. Verbs are the words for achieving action. Consider the totally different pictures created by these sentences: *He knocked down the door* and *He battered in the door. He shot the rabid raccoon with a .22-caliber rifle* and *He blasted the rabid raccoon between the eyes with a .22-dumdum bullet.*
5. Rely upon concrete word pictures rather than abstractions. This does not mean that you must separate all imagination from your thoughts. For example, Amos, the prophet of social justice in the Old Testament, did not give a long dissertation on the evils of prosperity attained through neglect of the underprivileged. He put the whole picture so concretely that no one could misunderstand. In effect he said to the rich, "I hate your beds of ivory, where you relax, singing and eating from flocks which you did not raise, while the faces of the poor are smeared with sweat and ground into the dust because of your luxuries." David did not say that Jonathan and Saul were brave and courage-

ous. He said "The bow of Jonathan turned not back, and the sword of Saul returned not empty." Robert Frost didn't have Silas, the hired man, say he was going to work hard. Frost had him say he was going to "ditch the meadow" and "clear the upper pasture."

An old Chinese axiom says, "One picture is worth a thousand words." Perhaps you can modify it slightly as a reminder to be concrete whenever possible: "One concrete word-picture is worth a thousand abstractions." Practice in selecting the concrete word is the first step toward effective use of the concrete word-picture.

6. Use modifiers only where a thought needs to be trimmed, enlarged, or given additional beauty, vividness, or action. Use modifiers which create sensory experiences to complete the understanding of an idea and to improve its image. Select modifiers that appeal to hearing as well as sight, taste as well as smell, touch as well as color, and feeling as well as motion.

Although we have dealt with only six principal ways to use words more effectively, you will discover many more if you use these six conscientiously. The words you select to express your thoughts have grave responsibilities. They must convey your knowledge and feeling, your character and sincerity, your respect for order and beauty, and your appreciation of clarity and understanding. Words are the raw material from which you must produce your most saleable product. Your listener and reader, the teacher who grades your recitation and paper, is looking for the best that you are capable of producing, expressed in words that he or she is capable of appreciating. When beauty can be fashioned from words, do not be content with dull and lifeless mediocrity. When excellence results from choosing the right labels for the word-pictures you are constantly creating, do not let excellence escape you.

CHAPTER 9

Spelling and Punctuation: Hallmarks of Completion

General spelling faults and how to correct them

Your vocabulary and the use you make of it depend to no small degree on your ability to spell. Many people have a speaking vocabulary much larger than their written one simply because they lack confidence in their ability to spell. Effective use of words also requires sufficient control of punctuation to keep words and thoughts in order. Perfection in spelling plus a thorough and consistent regard for the fundamental rules of punctuation will give your written work a hallmark of excellence.

You can improve your spelling by following several simple practices. Repeated tests have shown that the poor speller misspells a few words again and again. You can correct this fault quickly if you are willing to work at it. First note the words that you misspell most frequently. Keep a list of these words and go over them occasionally. When you add a word to the list, write it several times, emphasizing the part of the word you misspell by capitalizing the letters most often missed.

apitude	apTitude
seperate	sepArate
privelege	privIlege
litrature	litErature
Febuary	FebRuary
boundry	boundAry
ocassionaly	oCCasionaLLy

Close your eyes and visualize the trouble spot in capitals. Open your eyes briefly, then close them and visualize the word in small letters as it would appear on a printed page. Writing the word in small letters with your eyes closed is also recommended. This gives you the "feel" of the word.

A second spelling fault which you can correct with a little self-evaluation and awareness is carelessness. Why should anyone misspell these words: receive, too, all right, among, government, athlete, similar, surprise, break, or mountain? Yet these, and equally easy, often-used words have letters transposed, as in mount*ia*n—mountain, child*er*n—children; letters omitted, as in suprise— surprise, goverment—government; letters added, as in amo*u*ng—among, simil*i*ar—similar. Some words are carelessly used in place of the correct one, as *too* for *to* or *two*, *brake* for *break*, *accept* for *except*, *fourth* for *forth*, and *your* for *you're*. People who make these careless mistakes over and over assume that they know these words. Therefore, they will never bother to check the spelling or meaning of any of them in the dictionary. The way to correct these mistakes is to check and keep a second list. Head this list *Unnecessary Mistakes*, for a little awareness can correct this fault in a few days.

A third spelling fault results from mispronunciation. Although English is not always spelled phonetically (according to sound), a little observation on your part will usually reveal that your misspelling results from either adding or subtracting a syllable as you pronounce the word. Some people pay no attention to pronunciation marks even when they look up a word; others never sound out a word they are trying to spell. You can remedy this fault by paying attention to the pronunciation of words you habitually misspell and checking pronunciation marks as you check spelling in the dictionary. It may also help you to underline the syllable or letter you frequently add or omit.

labratory	laboratory
practicly	practically
disasterous	disastrous
rememberance	remembrance
hinderance	hindrance
enterance	entrance
intrest	interest

A fourth source of difficulty arises from the many homonyms in English. We met synonyms and antonyms in Chapter 7. Homonym comes from the Greek words *homas*, meaning *same*, and *onyma*, meaning *name*—thus, *same name*. Homonyms are words that have the same name (sound) but different meaning and spelling, as to, too, two—right, write, rite, wright—you, yew, ewe—and pair, pare, pear. You can correct misuse and misspelling by knowing the homonyms and their meanings. Here are some of the most misused:

aloud allowed	altogether all together	all ready already
alter altar	assent ascent	advise advice
bare bear	birth berth	born borne
bow bough	break brake	by buy
canon cannon	capitol capital	coarse course
corps corpse	compliment complement	council counsel
decent descent	dual duel	desert dessert
dear deer	fair fare	forth fourth
goal gold	grown groan	hear here
heir air	heal heel	him hymn
hole whole	herd heard	knew new
lesson lessen	led lead (metal)	meat meet
made maid	mist missed	pail pale
peace piece	peal peel	plain plane
pour pore	principal principle	profit prophet
seam seem	shown shone	steal steel
steak stake	stationary stationery	son sun

tale
tail

threw
through

their
there
they're

write
right
rite

to
too
two

weather
whether

Syllables and sound in correct spelling

Concern for the careless faults is, however, only the secondary consideration for correct spelling. The basic rules for the division of words into syllables, some sense of phonetics, and the spelling rules are all necessary. Knowledge of spelling rules is a great timesaver. The person who is forever checking the dictionary to find how a plural is formed, when a *y* changes to *i*, or when an *e* is dropped before a suffix spends an untold amount of valuable time on something that a little diligent study can accomplish for all time.

Syllables are parts of words which make one sound. The word *syllable* comes from the Latin and means *to hold together*. Thus, the letters that make up a single syllable are held together by sound—a single sound for each syllable. The following six rules for the division of words into syllables should be part of your everyday knowledge.

1. There are as many syllables in a word as there are vowels, except when two vowels are sounded as one or when the final *e* is silent. (In English there are many exceptions to rules, but careful observation can make the exception as familiar as the rule.) The vowel sounds are *a*, *e*, *i*, *o*, *u*, and *y* when it is sounded as *i*.

   Examples of Rule 1:

   Vocabulary, vo-cab-u-lar-y

Dictionary, dic-tion-ar-y (*io* is one sound)
Atmosphere, at-mos-phere (the final *e* is silent)
Two vowels making one sound: d*oe*s, l*oo*k, m*ea*n, r*ai*l, scr*ea*m
Silent *e* at the end of a word: alon*e*, glu*e*, hemispher*e*, improv*e*, hom*e*

2. If two consonants come between two vowels the syllables are usually divided between the consonants. (Consonants are the letters of the alphabet which are not vowels.)
   Examples of Rule 2:
   Mon-day, Tues-day, plun-der, pen-cil, may-be
3. When a consonant occurs between two vowels, the consonant goes with the second vowel unless the word is accented on the first syllable.
   Examples of Rule 3:
   be-fore, pri-mate, ar-bor, pa-per, va-cant
   Example of first syllable accent:
   vow-el, med-al, vol-ume, mod-el, giv-er
4. Words ending in *le* with a consonant before the *le* keep the consonant with the *le*, except for the consonant *k*.
   Examples of Rule 4:
   cir-cle, pur-ple, Bi-ble, un-cle, ea-gle
   Examples of *le* words with *k*:
   tack-le, pick-le, fick-le, buck-le, chuck-le
5. Double consonants are always split in syllable division.
   Examples of Rule 5:
   col-lege, pil-low, sil-ly, mid-day, let-ter
6. Prefixes and suffixes remain separate syllables when added to words, except *ed* unless it follows *t* or *d*.
   Examples of Rule 6:

en-close, re-cover, final-ly, hope-ful, mean-ness
Examples of *ed not* a separate syllable:
resign*ed*, cook*ed*, stepp*ed*, climb*ed*, fill*ed*.
Examples of *ed as* a separate syllable:
test-ed, dat-ed, plant-ed, collid-ed, prod-ded

Perhaps the number of exceptions noted above gives you cause to wonder. The answer to the question—Why so many exceptions?—is sound. The word *phonetics* comes from the Greek word *phone*, meaning to speak a sound. Your dictionary provides you with accent marks and their meaning. They need not be included here, but you should know them. You should also pay attention to the sounds which combined vowels produce. Spelling mistakes occur when two vowels are sounded as a single long vowel. Examples: br*ai*n (bran), tail (tal), clear (kler). Look up the following in your dictionary and remember what they mean: breve, macron, schwa, diacritical, digraph, and diphthong.

Rules and exceptions

The rules of spelling which follow will aid you in developing proper habits and establishing certain correct patterns:

1. Words which contain *ei* and *ie* follow a two-part rule. (a) Write *i* before *e* except after *c*.

Examples

ie	*ei*
bel*ie*ve	rec*ei*ve
rel*ie*f	rec*ei*pt
ach*ie*ve	c*ei*ling

(b) Write *ei* when the sound is *a*. Examples: weigh (way), neighbor (na-ber), freight (frat). Some exceptions are: either, weird, leisure, seize, protein.

2. When a suffix beginning with a vowel (able, ance, ed, ing, ist) is added, double the final consonant if the consonant is preceded by a single vowel which is accented.

Examples

begi*nn*ing	acqui*tt*ed
refe*rr*ing	occu*rr*ed
commi*tt*ed	occu*rr*ence
expe*ll*ed	allo*tt*ed
dru*gg*ist	swi*mm*ing

Exceptions occur when the suffix changes the accent. Examples: transfe*rr*ed (transfe*r*able), prefe*rr*ing (prefe*r*ence), refe*rr*ed (refe*r*ence). Exceptions also result from alternate accepted spellings. Examples: trave*l*ing (trave*ll*ing), worshi*p*ing (worshi*pp*ing), paralle*l*ed (paralle*ll*ed).

3. Words that end in a silent *e* drop the *e* if a suffix beginning with a vowel is added.

Examples

come–coming	dine–dining
desire–desirable	force–forcing
believe–believable	debate–debating

Exceptions occur in words ending in *ce* and *ge* when the suffix begins with *a* or *o*. Examples: peaceable, noticeable, courageous, serviceable. Exceptions also occur with some words ending in *e* when the suffix begins with a consonant. Examples: whole (wholly), true (truly), awe (awful), judge (judgment).

4. Words which end in *y* after a consonant change

the *y* to *i* when suffixes are added, except those suffixes beginning with *i*.

Examples

try–tries	carry–carries
dry–dries	apply–applies
vary–varied	notify–notified

Examples of suffix beginning with *i*: try–trying, rely–relying, worry–worrying, dry–drying, pity–pitying.

5. Words ending in *y* change the *y* to *i* for the *ly* suffix; those ending in *e*, except *le*, also add *ly*.

Examples of y to i

lazy–lazily	merry–merrily
temporary—temporarily	steady–steadily
satisfactory–satisfactorily	ordinary–ordinarily
late–lately	extreme–extremely
sincere–sincerely	definite–definitely

Exceptions occur when words end in *le*. The *e* is dropped and *y* added:

Examples

able–ably	gentle–gently
audible–audibly	subtle–subtly
reliable–reliably	double–doubly

6. Words ending in *l* add *ly*:

Examples

personal–personally	hopeful–hopefully
usual—usually	cruel–cruelly
awful–awfully	oral–orally

Spelling demons

There are other rules and other exceptions, but these six will help you form better habits of spelling.

The New York Board of Regents has prepared a list of the 100 words most often misspelled by high school students. As you study them, visualize how they are most frequently misspelled.

100 Simple Words Often Misspelled

ache
again
always
among
answer
any
been
beginning
believe
blue
break (to shatter)
built
business
busy
buy
can't
choose (present tense; *chose* is past tense)
color
coming
cough
could
country
dear
doctor
does
done
don't
early
easy
enough
every
February
forty
friend
grammar
guess
half
having
hear (ear)
heard
here (*there*—a place)
hoarse (frog in your throat)
hour
instead
just
knew
know
laid
loose (adjective and verb)
lose (verb—to *lose* money)
making
many
meant
minute
much
none
often
once
piece (a part of something)
raise
read (spelling is same for all tenses)
ready
said
says
seems
separate
shoes
since
some

Make a list of your own, starting with spelling demons from this selection. Add 300 words you commonly misspell. If you master your list of 300 troublesome words, you will probably be a better than average speller for the rest of your life. You will have evaluated your faults and developed habits to correct them.

After you have compiled your own list, compare

it with the following spelling demons which were misspelled most often on papers in a five-year test conducted at Kent School, Kent, Connecticut.

absence
accidentally
accommodate
accumulate
achievement
acknowledge
acquaintance
across
advice (noun)
advise (verb)
aggravate
all right
altogether
always
among
analysis
apparent
appearance
appropriate
arctic
argument
arrangement
ascend
assistant
association
athletics
audience
auxiliary
awful
awkward

beautiful
beginning
believe
benefit
boundary
breathe
bureau
business

changeable
college
coming
committee
comparatively
completely
conceive
conquer
conscience
conscious
convenience
convenient
copies
courageous
courteous
criticism
criticize
crowd
curiosity

defense
definite
describe
description
desirable
despair
desperate
develop
dining
disappear
disappoint
disastrous
discipline
disease
dissatisfied
divide
doctor
doesn't

ecstasy
excellent
exercise
exhaust
existence
explanation
extraordinary

familiar
fascinate
fatigue
February
finally
foreign
forty
fourth
friend
fulfill

generally
genius
government
governor
grammar
grateful
grievous
guarantee
guard
guardian
gymnasium

handkerchief
harass
height
heroes
hindrance
hoping
horizon
hospital
hurriedly
hypocrisy

calendar
campaign
candidate
captain
cemetery
certain

efficient
eighth
embarrass
equipped
especially
exaggerate

imagination
immediately
incidentally
independent
indispensable

infinite
initial
instance
intelligence
interest
interpret
irresistible
its

judgment

knowledge

laboratory
leisure
liable
license
lightning
likely
literature
loneliness
lonely
lose
lying

maintain
maintenance
maneuver
manual
marriage
mathematics
meant
medicine
medieval
merely
miniature
minimum
minute

neither
nickel
niece
nineteen
ninety
ninth
noticeable
nuisance

obedience
occasion
occasionally
occurred
occurrence
omission
omitted
opinion
opportunity
optimism
optimistic
orchestra
original
outrageous

pamphlet
parallel
parliament
particularly
pastime
peaceable
perceive
perform
perhaps
permanent
permissible
personally
personnel
perspiration

practically
preceding
preferred
prejudice
privilege
probably
procedure
proceed
professor
pronunciation
purpose
pursue

quantity
quiet
quite

realize
really
receive
recognize
recommend
referred
reign
relief
religious
repetition
representative
restaurant
rhythm
ridiculous
roommate

safety
satisfactorily
schedule
secretary
seize

mischievous
misspelled
movable
muscle
mysterious

necessary
necessity

persuade
physician
picnic
planning
portrait
portray
possess
possibility

sentence
separate
shining
siege
similar
sincerely
sophomore
specimen

speech
strength
strenuous
stretch
studying
subtle
succeed
success
successful
sufficient
supersede
superior
surely
surprise
syllable

tariff
temperament
thorough
thoroughly
tragedy
tremendous
truly
tyranny
Tuesday
twelfth

unanimous
undoubtedly
unnecessary
until
usually

vacuum
varieties
vegetable
vengeance
vicinity
villain

Wednesday
weird
welfare
wherever
wholly
women
writing
written

Summary of practices for spelling mastery

1. By self-examination find the few words you misspell again and again. Make a list of them and check it until you can recognize each troublemaker at a glance.
2. Correct the spelling fault of omitting, adding, and transposing letters in simple words by looking at the word. Many of the easiest words are misspelled because you have really never seen them.
3. Study pronunciation marks when you use the dictionary and form the habit of pronouncing words correctly. Pronounce all new words several times.

Divide them by syllables, consulting your dictionary if necessary.

4. Keep a handy list of the most confusing homonyms. Use it to avoid incorrect usage. Know the basic rules of spelling and keep one or two examples of each in mind.
5. Know the basic rules for dividing words into syllables, the vowel sounds, and the diacritical marks. Keep in mind two or three examples of each rule for syllable division.
6. Keep your own list of spelling demons. Study the 100 simple words most often misspelled. Compare your list of troublesome words with other lists. Note your weaknesses by checking the type of mistake you make: is it the *ei–ie* word, is it the *ly* suffix, is it the dropped *e*? Locate your specific weakness and correct it. Conscious awareness is often more than half the remedy.

The final word on spelling is probably *vision.* There are so many exceptions to rule and sound in English that perhaps a sense of keen perception is the one best practice in becoming a proficient speller. People who are able to recall what a page looks like, what is on it, etc., seem to make the best spellers. Perhaps to *really see* is to *succeed.*

The function of punctuation

We now turn to the last tiny dot and dash that will give your wisely selected, arranged, and correctly spelled words their clearest meaning—punctuation. The rules for the use of the period, the comma, the colon, the semicolon, the interrogation and exclamation points, the dash, apostrophe, and quotation marks plus the uses of parentheses, brackets, and the hyphen will not be given here. They are available in your English handbook and your dictionary.

Something of the history, nature, and usage of punctuation is probably both more interesting and more profitable. You must know the basic rules; these are your primary responsibility. We will concern ourselves with proper interpretation of the rules in order to make punctuation less arbitrary and more personal and meaningful.

The function of punctuation is to "slow down" or "stop." The word *punctuation* comes from the Latin word *punctus,* meaning a point. Thus, the different points (marks) of punctuation keep words from running away. In the "slowing" and "stopping" process, marks of punctuation replace gesture, changes of voice, pauses, and changes of thought.

Perhaps you have never tried to read a group of uncontrolled words. Read this tragic and moving picture of King David. David is an old man of about eighty. He has been a wonderful king, but some of his children have been bitterly disappointing. Absalom, a son whom he loved greatly, has been killed in battle. The old king has been so anxious for his son's safety that he has waited at the watchtower of the city gate for news of the battle. A messenger has just told David that Absalom is dead. The old king cannot believe it. He drags himself up the steps to the tower room. He will look and see Absalom riding. It is a gesture of hope but he knows it will not be.

See what you can make of the passage without punctuation:

And the King was deeply moved and went up to

the tower over the gate and wept and as he went he said o my son Absalom my son my son Absalom would I had died instead of you o Absalom my son my son.

Now read the same passage controlled by punctuation:

And the King was deeply moved, and went up to the tower over the gate, and wept; and as he went, he said, "O my son Absalom, my son, my son Absalom! Would I had died instead of you. O Absalom, my son, my son!"

Marks of punctuation are among those familiar everyday things which we take for granted. One of life's exciting learning processes is to ask questions about these familiar things. Did punctuation begin when writing began 3000 years ago? How did these little marks evolve?

Punctuation is not found in ancient writings. Ancient writing was in capital letters and words followed one after another without spacing. Punctuation as we know it is only about 500 years old, although separation marks appeared over 1000 years ago in some Hebrew, Greek, and Roman manuscripts. These first marks indicated little more than a stopping point of the scribe who was copying the manuscript. Priests also used a perpendicular line (|) to show them where to pause in their sermons. The first mark of punctuation used by the Greeks seems to have been the question mark (?). It was used as we use the semicolon (;). The Romans used the comma (,) and the colon (:). The Romans also introduced small letters but continued to capitalize each noun. Printing spread very rapidly throughout the Western world after the invention of movable type by Johann Gutenberg about

1450. (The Chinese had begun to print books by 105 A.D.) The first printers used a variety of punctuation marks. William Caxton, who set up the first printing press in England in 1476, used chiefly an oblique mark (/) and the perpendicular line (|); although the period (.) was already being used in England. The first book printed in the Western hemisphere (in Mexico City in 1539) used only the colon (:) and the period (.).

Punctuation as we use it, to control and show relationship among words, owes much to Aldus Manutius, who founded the famous Aldine press in Venice about the year 1500. Shakespeare seems to have understood the necessity of some punctuation. In *A Midsummer Night's Dream* three characters comment on the unpunctuated reading a character has given. First comment: "This fellow doth not stand upon points." Second: "He hath rid his prologue like a rough colt; he knows not the stop." Third: "His speech was like a tangled chain; nothing stopped, but all disorder." This play was written about the year 1594. When Shakespeare's plays were first printed in the year 1623, the period (.) occurred frequently. An English Grammar published in England, in the year 1633, gives rules for the use of the *stop*, the name given our *period*. Thus, it becomes plain that these little marks, accepted with dreariness and used without excitement, have biographies which are informative and pleasant to study.

Since the time of Aldus Manutius punctuation usage has changed much. People used to read everything aloud, so punctuation maintained a closer control than is necessary for rapid, silent reading. As people learned to read silently and to see more words at an eye fixation, punctuation did not need to control as strictly. Today modern writers use less punctuation than was the custom 100 years ago. Editors and generally accepted usage have established rules which are recognized as standard. At the same time punctuation usage is flexible enough to be personal to a degree. Whether you use close or loose punctuation is not of primary importance. First you must learn the rules which will give you the foundation of knowledge needed in order to make the proper judgments for effective control and relationship of words.[1]

The characteristics of the marks of punctuation

An understanding of the general nature or characteristics of the several marks of punctuation which are not self-explanatory, such as interrogation (question), exclamatory, and quotation marks, can add meaning to the rules of usage. The character of the *period* is to indicate a full stop. It implies a pause at the end of a unit of thought which stands alone.

Related to the period is the *semicolon*, whose nature is to indicate a "slowing down" between coordinate elements within a sentence. These coordinate elements are two clauses (related or parallel thoughts). The "slowing down" indicated by the semicolon may be compared to the slowing down of a car for the yellow traffic signal which occurs between the red and the green signals.

[1]Adapted from William H. Armstrong's *The Tools of Thinking: A Workbook* (Woodbury, N.Y.: Barron's Educational Series, Inc., 1965).

The *comma* is related to the semicolon in that it is a pause. However, it is much weaker, resembling in many respects a blinking caution light which demands less "slowing down." *Parentheses* and the *dash* sometimes replace the comma in setting off added words or ideas (called parenthetical material). The writer has certain freedoms in the use of each to achieve emphasis, variety, and to suit different conditions.

The nature of the *colon* is to indicate that something important is being introduced: (1) a significant explanation, (2) a long quotation, or (3) a list of words or groups of words.

One of the simplest of all the marks of punctuation is the apostrophe. Its uses are to show *possession* (John, John's; somebody, somebody's; Caesar, Caesar's); the *omission of letters* in words (doesn't, can't, won't, couldn't); and the *plural* of numbers, letters, words, and symbols (1960's, 1880's, 6's, k's, p's, m's, too's, and's, but's, M.D.'s, G.I.'s, V.I.P.'s). The apostrophe is the most neglected of all punctuation. Can it be that its uses are so easy that they are thought unimportant? Be sure that your written work is not marked CARELESS because you ignore the apostrophe. It is just as important as any other mark of punctuation.

Once you know the rules and understand the nature of punctuation, you should have no difficulty choosing, where choice is allowed, to suit your own style of writing and distinctive conditions. In an essay entitled *Guide to Usage*, Harrison Platt, Jr. gives a wonderful bit of advice that seems most fitting and proper for the conclusion of any discussion of punctuation.[2] "If a sentence is very difficult to punctuate," he writes, "so as to make the meaning clear, the chances are that the arrangement of words and ideas is at fault. The writer will do better if he rearranges his word order instead of wrestling with his punctuation."[2]

Summary for enlightened punctuation

1. Appreciate the basic function of punctuation–to give your written word its final clarification.
2. Know the rules that govern the use of punctuation marks.
3. Add interest to what might seem a rather drab study by knowing something of the history and development of punctuation.
4. Know the nature and general character of the several punctuation marks, particularly those which perform related functions.
5. Use the freedom allowed the writer, within the rules, to make your punctuation personal and a part of your individual writing style.
6. Always remember that if punctuation cannot clarify, change the word arrangement.

[2]*The American College Dictionary*, published by Random House. *Guide to Usage*, by Harrison Platt, Jr., found in the back of dictionary.

CHAPTER 10

Books: The Memory of Mankind

The escape hatch from savagery

Books should never be defined as assembled pages of printed words bound together and enclosed in hard or soft bindings. Neither pages nor printing have anything to do with the definition of books. The books, over a million of them, which Ptolemy Philadelphus collected in Alexandria before the dawn of the Christian era were in the form of clay tablets, parchment squares, and papyrus rolls. The library, which the Assyrian king, Ashurbanipal, collected in Nineveh 600 years before the birth of Christ, was composed chiefly of clay tablets. This library lay under the sands for 2000 years—waiting for the archeologist's cautious shovel. The long rolls, or scrolls, discovered by a fifteen-year-old Bedouin shepherd in a cave on the rugged hills overlooking the Dead Sea did not resemble what we would describe physically as books; however, they are books. Stored in the caves by ancient Hebrew scholars who fled Jerusalem to escape the Romans, the Dead Sea scrolls preserved for nearly 2000 years a sacred segment of the memory of mankind.

It is therefore apparent that the essential nature of books has nothing to do with their physical form. They are not chemically treated wood pulp covered with printer's marks. Neither does the nature of books have anything to do with the particular kind of material that is contained in them—be it fiction or nonfiction, drama or essay, poetry or prose. The correct definition of books must be a generic definition; that is, it must be all inclusive.

Before we find the correct definition let's look briefly at the condition of primitive man before he learned to read and write. Each new generation had to learn almost everything over again. From the beginning man had been set apart from the other animals by his distinguishing characteristic of memory Certain animals are capable of remembering various things for varying lengths of time, but anything approaching the transmission of memory among animals comes under the heading of instinct.

As generation after generation of primitive people learned everything over again, one tremendous development was slowly taking place. Primitive man was learning to record his memory; he was learning to read and write. He learned to record what he knew, what he thought, what he felt, and what he had done. He remains the only creature who records his memory, and the thousands of years of accumulated memory are what books are. They are the dynamic, vital, and irresistible force that enabled man to blast away the escape hatch of dark superstition and ignorance and flee from savagery.

Books are the memory of mankind. In them are recorded the accumulated knowledge of mankind—the acts and discoveries, dreams and inventions, myths and thoughts, feelings and passions—all that has become real and all that ever stirred the human mind. They have enriched human life over the centuries; they push back the boundaries of our ignorance; they allow us to become a part of the human community, rather than be isolated in the narrow experience of one lifetime. Books lead us realistically and rationally into the past and speculatively with vision, hope, and confidence into the future. They present cases from yesterday upon which we can formulate judgments today and ideals for tomorrow. They stir us up and cause us to take a second look at things we have taken for granted. Books are, apart from the effort and influence of a good teacher, the chief source of education, and through them the student explores the richness of human experience and the wisdom of the ages.

Have you ever stopped to think what our world would be like without books? Sit quietly for ten minutes (time yourself) and try to think of as many things as you can that would not be available to you were it not for books. You will never again feel the same about books. The textbooks you have sometimes wanted to be rid of take on new meaning; they become a part of a treasure without which we might not be called human.

Using books wisely

Now that we have learned what books are and how

vital they are to our lives, let us see how we can use them wisely and profitably. Whether you use a book for assignment or pleasure, getting acquainted is the first step toward both appreciation and understanding. If you knew you were going to spend several hours, days, or weeks with another person, you would want to find out all you could about him or her. Yet students sometimes spend a whole year with a textbook and the two remain strangers.

One excellent approach to a book is to ask yourself questions about it. Why did the author write it? What would you have done differently in dealing with the same subject? Could it have been given a better title? What is the meaning of the designs on the cover? Why were these particular illustrations chosen? Many readers pay no attention to the parts of a book. They go directly to the contents, missing much that would add significantly to their understanding and interest.

When you begin a book you should note these parts: title, author, imprint, copyright, printings, foreword, preface, table of contents, list of illustrations, sometimes an introduction in addition to the preface, usually a translator's note if the book is translated from a foreign language, chapter titles, often subdivision heads, notes, appendixes, sometimes defining or pronouncing glossaries, bibliography, and index. Of course, all these are not found in a novel, but a well-written textbook contains most of these parts; all should be carefully studied.

A test question—What is the full title of your textbook and who is the author?—revealed that eight people out of thirty did not know the full title of a book they had been studying for four months; seventeen of the thirty did not know the author. When you begin a book note the minor parts. If a note of information gives the qualifications of the author read it carefully. This, plus a thorough reading of the preface, should put you on a personal footing with the author.

The preface is a statement of the author's purpose, the plan of the book, and frequently it tells the reader how the book can best be used. Often a foreword, written by someone other than the author, precedes the preface. Sometimes the foreword is written by a well-known authority on the subject of the book to give the book prestige. You should always read it, however, for often the writer will indicate a difference in point of view which can prove helpful to the reader as he develops his own thoughts on the subject. An introduction may replace the preface or be included with the preface. If both are included, the introduction usually explains the book's broad aims and sometimes summarizes the subject matter.

Your second important pause when beginning a book should be at the table of contents. You should quickly review the table of contents of a textbook at frequent intervals during the term. The reasons for this are obvious. Here is an outline of what the book contains. Here on a single page or two the relationship of parts of the subject is arranged for you. At examination time this bird's-eye view can help you coordinate the course material, particularly those parts which may be used for essay questions. For the general reader, the table of contents may indicate whether or not the subject matter is that which interests him. For example, a reader interested in the American West would quickly learn from the table of contents that William H. McNeill's *The Rise of the West* was not about the American West, but a history of Western civilization.

After entering the book by the front door, the reader goes to the back to check bibliography, notes, appendixes, glossary, and index. The bibliography lists the sources to which the author has gone for material, authoritative books related to the subject, and perhaps "suggested books" for further reading. Your ability to critically evaluate a bibliography may aid your judgment regarding the thoroughness of the author's research.

Appendixes are added to explain more fully or to include material pertinent to the text but not necessarily a part of it. The word appendix comes from the Latin *appendere*, meaning *to attach.*

Glossaries may give pronunciation of difficult names. A glossary is sometimes included in Greek history texts, for Greek names are difficult for the beginner. In scientific, technical, and highly specialized books the glossary usually includes definitions which relate specifically to the subject matter or those not likely to be found in an abridged dictionary. The word glossary comes from the Greek word *glossa,* meaning *to explain a word* or tongue (language).

The index is really the back door to a book. It contains an alphabetical list, usually cross-referenced, of the items in the book. You can use it to quickly find any significant name, reference, or topic included in the book. Indexes are usually not found in books of imaginative writing, such as novels and poetry. They are, however, indispensable to books of detailed exposition.

Although it may have seemed foolish to you when we started, examination of these frequently overlooked parts of a book should appear invaluable, especially when the reader wishes to choose the best from among several books on the same subject. Your teachers made a thorough study of all the parts of several texts in each subject before the one you are studying was chosen. As you get to know your books, see if you can determine the qualities which influenced your teacher's choice.

You should now be sufficiently acquainted with the book to find further aids to understanding in the contents itself. Observe chapter titles and subdivision headings. If the author has chosen his words to announce clearly what the chapter contains, you will be directed on the "right path." Even a novel with chapter titles, rather than chapter numbers, is more attractive to most readers.

Some books are arranged with chapter introductions set in italics or smaller type. You should read these carefully after you have read the chapter title itself. Frequently such an introduction clarifies the topic. In good translations of many classics, such as those by Homer, Dante, and Goethe, a brief survey of what the chapter contains is included as an aid to the reader. This is especially true of translations in poetry form. Some authors introduce a chapter with a short, topical quotation from another writer. These, plus subdivision headings, illustration captions, footnotes, and end-of-chapter notes all require more than a passing glance by the reader.

Making books serve your special needs

Perhaps you can best determine the use you wish

to make of a book by asking questions. Is this the book on the subject that I want? Is it too advanced or too elementary? What do I want to get out of it? What does it offer that will be valuable to me? These questions relate, of course, chiefly to nonfiction books. Your personal tastes will prompt questions regarding fiction, poetry, and other reading which you do for pleasure.

The reader with intellectual curiosity uses each book to get exactly what he or she wants from it and no more. There are four general reasons which cover most uses of books: (1) to get information; (2) to improve one's ability to think; (3) for personal and professional development; and (4) for the sheer joy of reading. The person who is capable of wise judgment gets the best from many books instead of everything from a few. There are many dull books and you will have to read some of them while you are in school. However, if you know what you are looking for and if you are intellectually curious, you will often discover more than you thought the book had to offer.

"Light from two sources," says an old axiom, "is the way to get rid of shadows." This is especially true in the use of books. Teachers often suggest to students who are finding a subject difficult and uninteresting that they read one or two general or related books on the subject. The results are usually what the teacher anticipated—renewed interest and new light (understanding). The student who hates biology reads a biography of the great naturalist Louis Agassiz or Charles Darwin's adventures during the scientific exploration of the South Seas, aboard the *Beagle*, and biology becomes a favorite subject. A student who finds American history dull, and his textbook filled with one difficult maze of facts after another, reads Oscar Hamlin's life of William Lloyd Garrison and two or three chapters from one of Dr. Samuel Eliot Morison's books. He learns the secret of bringing American history to life—first use the book for the general reader; then use the textbook. Twice as much is learned with half the effort, and "light from two sources" has dispelled the shadows of dullness. Students in a beginning Latin class thought it very strange that their first assignment was to read a little book about Romans entitled *Roman Panorama*.[1] They wondered later why so many students from other classes, but no one from their class, dropped Latin. The teacher knew. *Roman Panorama* gave a readable, entertaining picture of the everyday life and customs of the Romans. When the students met the first Latin words they knew the people who had spoken them.

Reading experience and discovery

Your ability to use books to the best advantage will increase as you practice looking for something. Sometimes it is better to read quickly two or three books on a subject without trying to remember all the details than to study one book thoroughly. Try to use books so that both the forest and the trees are revealed to you.

When you begin to use books to supplement your knowledge of either a school subject or of something which interests you, don't be afraid to start small. Don't select a big book, filled with detail and intended for the specialist. Start with a small book written for

[1]Humphrey Grose-Hodge, *Roman Panorama* (New York: Macmillan Co., 1947).

the general reader. A short introductory work will give you the essentials and a sense of proportion. It will probably stimulate you to pursue the study further; the exhaustive and detailed work might make you lose interest.

One of the most satisfying uses of books is not to accumulate knowledge of times past and lands, people, and nations; but to give one insight into the problems of good and evil, of love and hate, of life and death, and of happiness and misery. Great books deal with the knowledge of all time—and the problems of everyday life have remained about the same throughout the ages. Great books provide a means of conversation with the superior minds of all ages—the wisest counselors, the most learned philosophers, the able and sprightly poets and fablists who can make one laugh.

At no time in history has this glorious memory of mankind been as accessible as it is now. The paperback industry has made it possible for you to buy both the worst and the best of this memory. Unfortunately, the impression prevails that the best books, called classics, are often dull and always difficult to read. The word "classic" comes from the Latin *classicus*, meaning superior. Originally it referred to a class of citizens; now it is used to describe that which has withstood time and the critics. If you choose a classic, your conversation with the writer is likely to be exciting, clear, and meaningful; you will find it neither dull nor difficult to read. When you have finished you will have stood on the shoulders of a giant and you will have widened your horizon.

Just as there is no end to the production of books,

there is no end to their use. While you are still in school they will help you learn more about your subjects and, therefore, improve your grades. Throughout your life they will help you build self-confidence, self-reliance, and a better way of life.

Summary of practices for getting more from books

1. Use the separate parts of a book to get acquainted with the author, his plan, and his writing.
2. Use questions to determine the use you wish to make of a particular book.
3. Use a book to get exactly what you desire from it. Looking for a particular thing will usually reveal that and more.
4. Use a book designed for the general reader to better understand your school subjects. Do not be afraid to start small by using a short introductory work.
5. Use a book that reveals both the forest and the trees. It might be more valuable to quickly survey two or three volumes on a subject than to study one book in detail. Practice will aid you in making such judgments.
6. Consider the great books, the "classics," as friends who offer wise counsel and direction toward a fuller and better life.

CHAPTER 11

Reading: Faster with More Understanding

The nature of reading

"Reading is to the mind what exercise is to the body," wrote Joseph Addison, the great English essayist, in 1711. Our study of words achieves nothing unless we put words together to make thoughts. Unless we enrich our thoughts by the great legacy of thought put in books, our minds miss the exercise needed for development. As knowledge of words improves one's reading, so reading improves one's knowledge of words; for words are the tools of thinking, and reading is the storehouse from which comes most of our thinking.

In dealing with the effective attack upon an assignment we mentioned some aspects of reading. We indicated the three objects of a good reader: (1) to concentrate on what is being read; (2) to remember as much as possible; and (3) to apply or associate what is read to one's own experience. We also named the three general types of reading: (1) Skimming—this is quick scanning to find a particular fact. Skimming may also mean rapid reading to find the main idea without gathering accompanying details. (2) Careful reading—this is directed toward finding the main topics, fixing them in mind, judging the important details, and relating them to the main topics. (3) Intensive reading—this is used when total understanding is required. Technical material, instructions in textbooks and on tests, and cumulative textbook information require intensive reading.

These types refer chiefly to reading to complete an assignment rather than reading for pleasure, although anyone who has a desire to learn probably reads with a great degree of pleasure all the time. All practices for the development of better reading habits deal in one way or another with three aspects: (1) what to look for; (2) how to improve comprehension; and (3) how to increase speed. It soon becomes apparent that the different practices are generally variations rather than separate approaches. After you have studied the suggestions for improving these three aspects of reading, you can choose and modify them according to your individual needs. Perhaps you can think of new methods which will serve you better. If you are like the great majority of readers, your first and most difficult task will be to convince yourself that you can improve your reading habits. The almost universal attitude is that after the formal reading instruction of our first four or five years of elementary school, we *know how to read.* With these words we consider the judgment definite and further investigation unnecessary.

Reading is an extremely complex mental-visual-psychological process, difficult to learn, impossible to do efficiently without continued conscientious effort, but able to be improved throughout one's lifetime. Reading is a challenge, and when done successfully, it is an adventure which involves two persons–the reader and the author. The reader must carry on a silent conversation with the author, asking what he is saying, questioning his reasons, and approving or disapproving of the manner in which he presents his material. Reading is never passive acceptance. It is an energy-absorbing activity which requires movement of the reader's mind to meet the mind of the author and to grasp the meaning of his thoughts.

Henry David Thoreau, in *Walden*, or *Life in the Woods*, includes an essay on reading. *Walden*, available in several paperback editions, is an excellent book to use to improve your reading skills. Thoreau says (the italics are the author's):

> ***To read well—that is, to read true books in a true spirit—is a*** **noble exercise,** ***and one that will*** **task the reader more than an exercise** ***which the customs of the day esteem.*** **It requires** ***a*** **training** ***such as the*** **athletes underwent, the steady intention almost** ***of the*** **whole life** ***to this object.*** **Books must be read as deliberately and reservedly as they were written.**[1]

[1]Henry David Thoreau, *Walden* or *Life in the Woods* (The Heritage Press, 1939), p. 107.

In the same essay he continues:

The works of the great poets have never yet been read by mankind, for only great poets can read them. They have only been read as the multitude read the stars, at most astrologically, not astronomically. Most men have learned to read to serve a paltry convenience, as they have learned to cipher {count} in order to keep accounts and not be cheated in trade; but **of reading as a noble intellectual exercise they know little or nothing, yet this only is reading in a high sense,** ***not that which lulls us as a luxury and suffers the nobler faculties to sleep the while, but*** **what we have to stand** ***on tip-toe to read and*** **devote** ***our*** **most alert** ***and*** **wakeful** ***hours to.***[2]

What to Look For

The first step in improving reading ability is to know what to look for. How can you best train your-

[2]*Ibid.*, p. 110.

self to look for ideas and thoughts rather than words? Words are the labels used to portray the writer's thoughts, but you do not take the words from the printed page. Ideas and thoughts (idea is used here to designate a portion of a thought) are removed from the page; consequently, they are what you must train yourself to find. The best way to train yourself to read for thoughts and ideas is to begin by getting a quick bird's-eye view of the material.

Turn back to the quotations from Thoreau. Do not plod from word to word. Skim rapidly over the passages and try to pick up from the italicized sections the main thought: Reading is a noble intellectual exercise, requiring more training than most people are willing to devote to it. Now go back and enjoy reading the entire passage. The facts will not become jumbled and confusing, and the organization and purpose will stand out clearly.

Since it is obvious that the best way to obtain a bird's-eye view is to read rapidly the core of the paragraph, each paragraph indentation should alert the reader. Going over the paragraph quickly for the central thought prevents the reader from creeping up on each word, or as it sometimes seems, from waiting for the word to crawl to the reader. This practice also gives the reader an awareness of thoughts. This may be compared to first looking at the forest and then approaching to look at the trees. Returning to pick out the contributing ideas from the individual sentences is comparable to looking at the trees. However, no one looks at every tree in the forest; only significant ones are observed. This procedure can be remembered by the formula:

$$P + S = CT$$

Paragraph + Sentence = Complete Thought

You will note that this formula for what to look for in reading has no *W* for *words*. You will, of course, see words, but only as necessary labels for ideas. They will no longer be the purpose for reading.

Knowing what to look for in reading assumes a basic knowledge of paragraph patterns and sentence structure. The reader must be able to see instantly what a paragraph is, how it is developed, where the topic sentence is, and what ideas are contained in the sentences. The four basic characteristics of all paragraphs are exposition, description, narration and argumentation. These basic forms of discourse may be arranged in various patterns of paragraphs: (1) question and answer; (2) comparison and contrast; (3) cause and effect; (4) opinion and proof; (5) repetition of example; and (6) multiplication of details. Variations of these patterns can be found in your English handbook. One or two examples will show you how quickly comprehension follows if you know exactly what you are looking for.

Here is a question and answer paragraph (the italics are the author's):

How should you read? *As you please. If you please yourself by reading fast, read fast; if you read slowly and do not feel like reading faster, read slowly. Pascal does not say we are apt to read too fast or too slowly, but he blames only an excess.*

(Levity is foolish to read too fast, but seriousness will be a gainer in many cases if it reads briskly.) Montaigne complains of a formal way of reading. "My thoughts go to sleep when they are seated," he says, "so they and I walk." Honest industry merely jogs along, curiosity flies on Mercury's pinions. Passionate reading not only flies, it skips, but it does so only because it can choose, which is a high intellectual achievement. How do you read the time-table? You skip till you come to your place; then you are indifferent to the whole world and engrossed by your train, its departure, arrival, and connections. The same thing with a map which a motorist lends the anxious cyclist at the crossroads. The latter's whole soul is in his reading. The same thing with any formula for the production of the philosopher's stone. **Whatever we read** ***from*** **intense curiosity** ***gives us the*** **model of how we should always read. Plodding along page after page** ***with an equal attention to each word***

results in attention to mere words. Attention *to* words never produces thought, *but very promptly results in distractions, so that an honorable effort is brought to nought by its own ill-advised conscientiousness.*[3]

It is highly probable that the reader who reads only words would read the question at the beginning of the paragraph without really seeing it. Such a reader would lose the whole paragraph, for there can be no answer without a question.

Note the essentials of the topic sentence in this expository paragraph (again the italics are the author's):

***Among the many kinds of material we must find in books, at least* three *are readily distinguished:* happenings, facts, *and* principles. *Happenings—the narratives of* what *has* occurred—*concerns us in* all forms *of* fiction, *whether as plays, novels, or stories. And* happenings *are a* major part *of all* history *and* biog-**

[3]Ernest Dimnet, *The Art of Thinking* (New York: Simon and Schuster, 1928).

raphy. *Throughout such narratives and in almost all* sorts of writing *we encounter* facts *which may lack narrative connection: dates, names, locations, definitions, descriptions of processes. Less concrete than either happenings or facts, and often* harder *to* remember, *are* principles: *the* translation *of* facts into *statements of* law, *the* interpretation *of* happenings *as* cause *and* effect, *or the attempts to explain* human experience *in the* form *of* theories.[4]

The topic sentence alerts the reader; the signal word, *three*, gives the clue. The body of the paragraph explains what *happenings*, *facts*, and *principles* are. The reader who knows what to look for will not have to reread this paragraph.

Here is a summary paragraph to help you remember what to look for in your reading.

Summary Paragraph

What does the good reader look for as he reads? First, for thoughts. Secondly, the reader looks for action on a wide screen—he moves quickly over the page and gets a bird's-eye view. Thirdly, he knows the

[4]E. Wayne Marjarum, *How to Use a Book* (New Brunswick, N.J.: Rutgers University Press, 1947).

forms of discourse, patterns of paragraphs, and structure of sentences so thoroughly that they almost jump from the page to meet the reader. Finally, the reader selects and classifies the kinds of material found in books—happenings, facts, and principles. What the good reader looks for in his reading causes him to think; all effective reading is thinking.

Understanding more

The second major area that concerns us is how to comprehend more of what we read and remember it longer.

The first step toward greater comprehension and longer retention is *purpose*. You must have a clear realization of your objectives. Aim to coordinate your purpose with the purpose of the writer. In an essay entitled *A Teacher Looks at Reading*, A. B. Herr classifies the purposes of writers under three major divisions: "(1) to give information—an intellectual operation; (2) to share experiences, sentiments, and convictions—an operation which includes intellectual comprehension but is not complete without emotion, the feeling of having participated; and (3) to persuade, to change opinions, responses, or habits—an operation whose success depends on emotional acceptance, no matter how intellectual the approach may appear."

The nature of your assignment will generally dictate the purpose. Once the purpose has been established the reader will decide whether to use skimming, careful reading, or intensive reading, or a combination. If your purpose is to locate information, skimming will suffice. If your purpose is to gather facts and understand their interrelationship, and to form opinions which are backed by substantial evidence, you may have to follow your skimming with careful or intensive reading.

A second way to achieve better comprehension and easier retention is to condition your mind for positive rather than negative results. Many readers who are faced with a difficult passage or assignment start by expecting *not* to be able to understand and remember it. This prepares their minds psychologically for defeat. Expect to understand and remember. Tell yourself: "I am going to remember this after one reading." Would the runner win the race if at the starting gun he said to himself, "I know I can't win"? Would the hurdler clear the hurdle if he said just before he left the ground, "I know I won't clear it"? Purpose plus confidence will help increase your comprehension and retention.

A third aid to comprehension and retention is to read with questions in mind. The right questions can help the reader make the information so personal that it is impossible to forget it. What would you have done at the Battle of Thermopylae? Would you have enjoyed walking and talking with Milton as he felt his way along his garden path with his cane? Could the author have stated this rule more clearly? What could I use as a more precise example? "There is no such thing as an interesting book or assignment"; to paraphrase Emerson, "there are only interested readers." We might add that only interesting questions make interested readers. How is this assignment related to the preceding one? Will what I already know about the topic make it easier for me to remember the facts I am now learning? When you finish a section or chapter, self-recitation questions about the main topics and how successfully (or unsuccessfully) the author has presented them will increase your ability to remember more of what you have read.

You can retain what you read by finding some unifying association or significance. Facts and ideas alone can be very dull; however, if you can establish some relationships, either logically or arbitrarily, you will find that the facts and ideas make a convenient package of information.

Remembering Longer

Much of the reading done in school introduces the learning skill which always causes students to shudder—memorization. You need not fear this word. Perhaps you would have a clearer understanding of much that you have to read if your teacher did not try to avoid using it by substituting phrases such as "learn all" or "learn the whole ten rules."

The first step in improving your powers of memory and putting them to work in your reading is to find out which kinds of ideas you remember with less difficulty than others—whether happenings, facts, or principles, and the element in each that helps you remember. Some people remember color, others motion, still others cannot remember numbers when they are spelled out. General U. S. Grant could not remember the names of three consecutive towns he marched through, but on a topographical map he could memorize dozens of towns and their location in a matter of seconds. Alexander the Great could not remember the names of some of his close acquaintances, but he could memorize poetry with almost no effort.

Psychologists generally agree that each of us has not one memory power but many. By finding what we remember more easily, whether it is *faces, places, dates, designs, pictures from reality, pictures from imagination,* or *association with the physical or mental world,* we can find our memory strengths and use them as the association frames upon which to hang what we must remember.

One very simple but effective test is to think quickly of someone you met recently. How do you remember him? By what he was doing? By the place where you saw him first? By who was with him? By the color of his shirt or jacket? By some number—books he was carrying, steps forward to shake hands, words spoken? By what he really looked like? (reality). By what you thought he might have looked like? (imagination). Which do you remember more distinctly—his handshake? (physical)—or what he said? (mental). Apply the same test to a character you have met in your reading.

When you find that association and memory are not sufficient because you have so many facts to remember, your last recourse is to take notes. If you own the book you are reading, making marginal notes and designating important points by a suitable and consistent system of marking are invaluable.

One of the simplest methods of designating degrees of importance is to use one, two, or three vertical lines: | for important, || for very important, and ||| for "must remember." Some students use a (?) question mark to indicate "further study needed"; some use *T* or *Ex.* to signal probable test or examination material. One good practice is to write the main thought of a paragraph in a brief question beside the paragraph. Some students try to include a brief summary at the end of each paragraph.

Note-taking on what you read forces you to think and to be constantly alert for the essentials. Your notes will be in better order and available for quicker use if you take them on 3″ x 5″ index cards. You can file them by subject or book, and you can arrange them far more easily than looseleaf notebook material.

A review of summary writing and outlining will afford you two methods of taking notes on what you read. Two additional types of reading notes are also sometimes used: (1) question and answer; and (2) word and phrase list. The question and answer method states the question in full and indicates the answer with key words or phrases. For example:

I. What does a good summary contain?
   A. Principal ideas
   B. Author's point of view
   C. Student's vocabulary

II. What are the steps in making a summary?
   A.
   B.
   C.

The question and answer method sharpens your attentiveness and enforces the questioning attitude. Once practiced it leads to clear-cut distinctions between major and minor topics.

The word and phrase list form of notes is little more than an unorganized outline. It is used most often for reviewing quickly for tests. It offers a series of warning signals which remind the reader what to remember. For example, here is a quick review of this chapter:

Reading: Faster with More Understanding
Look for
Bird's-eye view
Thoughts
Main topics
Comprehension
Writer's aim
Questions on material
Happenings
Facts
Principles
Retention
Memory powers
Application and association
Marginal notes
Written notes
Increasing Speed
Self-tests
Conscious purpose
Hollow triangle
Mechanics
Cautions

Note that words indicating principal parts are in italics. You probably should reserve the word and phrase list form of notes for more informal and less demanding subject matter.

Reading faster

The third principal area for improvement in reading is the speed at which you read. It is now an established fact that fast readers are more accurate and remember more than slow readers. They also have the advantage of saving much time. The slow reader loses his train of thought and often his place on the page; the fast reader reads several words at a glance and deals only in thoughts. Many self-tests are available for measuring your reading and comprehension. Your English teacher can either provide you with or administer such a test. Find out how fast you read and how much you comprehend of what you read. If you have reading difficulties, the test will probably pinpoint areas where specific practices can help.

How do we read? First of all, every reader faces the problem of coordinating the mind and the eye. The mind is capable of receiving ideas much more rapidly than the eye is able to receive and relay them. Thus, the problem of mind-wandering arises. If we do not discipline the mind to remain ready, it escapes to thoughts of ourselves, friends, what we are going to do later—and suddenly we have lost our place on the page. The slower you read, the more difficulty you will have in controlling the mind; therefore by reading rapidly you are training the eye to speed up and the mind to accept the eye's pace.

Our eyes move across the page by a series of quick stops, not in a flowing, even movement. These stops are called fixations; whether we see one word or several at a fixation determines our speed of reading. The fast reader, who will always remember more of what he reads than the slow reader, makes two or three fixations as he reads the line of print, and he sees groups of words, ideas, and thoughts. The slow reader usually interrupts the forward movement across the page to glance backward. This bad and confusing habit is called "regression" and results from reading without sufficient purpose and speed. The good reader sweeps from the end of the finished line downward and to the beginning of the next with no difficulty; the slow reader will often make two or three false starts before beginning a line and frequently reread the line just read or skip the one he should read. This, of course, is not completely the fault of the eye. Until the eye and the brain are working together, all these sloppy reading habits prevail. Mechanical practices will help, but the determined effort to concentrate on increasing speed and comprehension, and a willingness to make each assignment a practice in better reading habits, will prove your greatest aid.

One mechanical aid to measure your "recognition span," the number of words you see at a fixation, may be recommended. From cardboard or some other semi-stiff material cut out a hollow triangle. Make the base wide enough to take in six or eight words. Place it on a line and move it from top to bottom to determine how many words you see at a fixation. Use the triangle for a few minutes' practice each day or as a test from time to time to measure your improvement. You can also use a chart to note the number of pages (of similar material) that you can read in a 15-minute period. If you put serious effort into reading improvement, this test can be done weekly.

Careful self-analysis of your capacities will dictate your methods. Be cautious about developing speed with comprehension. Nervous haste without understanding will produce no beneficial results. Let the purpose determine the speed. If you concentrate on correcting the obvious faults of the slow reader, your speed will probably increase automatically.

Keep three things in mind: (1) All study problems are really reading problems. (2) Improvement in reading is a lifetime process. (3) If we read, we can become better readers; if we do not read, we become increasingly poorer readers.

Summary of practices for better reading

1. Prepare the mind psychologically for positive results.
2. Know the three aims of a good reader: (1) to concentrate on what you are reading; (2) to remember as much as possible; and (3) to apply or associate what you read to your own experience.
3. Know the three general types of reading and the type of material to which each may be best applied: (1) skimming; (2) careful reading; and (3) intensive reading.
4. Know that the good reader looks for: (1) thoughts; (2) bird's-eye view; (3) main topics; and (4) pattern and structure in picturing ideas.
5. Understand the approaches to better comprehension and retention: (1) Reading is a conversation with the author. (2) Always know the purpose for which you are reading. (3) Always read with questions in mind. (4) Use your memory powers to improve your retention by association and application. (5) Make use of written notes.
6. Make a determined effort to increase your speed of reading: (1) Use self-tests to measure your speed and rate of improvement. (2) Know the

mechanical functions of the eye in reading. (3) Keep in mind the faults of the slow reader. (4) Know that fast readers remember more of what they read than slow readers. (5) Discipline the eye to take in more at a fixation. (6) Remember that speed without understanding is useless.

CHAPTER 12

The Library: How to Use It

How to find a book

In Chapter 4 we suggested that your school library or a public library provides both atmosphere and incentive for serious study, and that if you do not have satisfactory conditions at home, the library habit could become one of your best study habits. One of the most important rooms or buildings at your school and in your town or city is the library. This chapter will tell you what is available and how to find what you want in the library.

Knowing the parts of a book—title, author, publisher, date of publication, and edition—is the first step toward finding what you want in the library. Once you know this information you are prepared to find out if the book you want is in the library. For this you use the card catalogue.

The card catalogue is not a catalogue in book form. It is a series of drawers labeled with letters of the alphabet. All cards are filed alphabetically, beginning with the first important word of the title—*A*, *An*, and *The* are omitted. In addition to the title card there are also author and subject cards. However, the title card is the quickest to use if you know what book you want.

Example of title card:

Audubon bird guide.
Pough, Richard H.
598.2 Audubon bird guide; eastern land birds.
P Doubleday, 1946.

Suppose you read the book and decide that you enjoy the author and would like to read some more of his works if such exist. You return the book you have read to the library and check the *author card* for additional books. There will be a separate author card for each work of the author. As an example let us imagine you have read John Kieran's *An Introduction to Birds* and are checking the author cards for more books by him. On the author card his name will be listed as *Kieran, John*. If the library has his *Birds of New York City*, it will be listed first. The next author card will probably list *Footnotes on Nature*; the third will be the book you have just returned, *Introduction to Birds*, with the article *An* omitted. The author card usually gives the most complete information on the book, although it may contain the same facts as the other cards.

Example of author card:

598.2 Pough, Richard H.
P Audubon bird guide; eastern land birds.
Doubleday, 1946.
Birds
t.

Suppose you wish to study birds but you do not know authors or titles. A third card is available to help you. It is called the *subject card,* and may be indexed as a general subject (BIRDS) or a specific subject (SONG BIRDS). Subject cards are either printed with the subject in capitals or in red to distinguish them.

Example of subject card:

BIRDS
598.2 Pough, Richard H.
P Audubon bird guide; eastern land birds.
Doubleday, 1946.

Subject card (more complete)

AMERICAN FOLKWAYS
917.63 Kane, Harnett Thomas 1910–
K Deep Delta Country, Duell, 1944.
XX, 283 p. maps. Selected bibliography
pp. 273–80.

Subject cards are not included for fiction except for historical novels of recognized merit.

You cannot remove the file to show the librarian what you want. You must copy (sometimes special forms are provided) the following information: (1) call number, (2) author's name, (3) title, (4) volume and edition, and (5) your own name.

You have probably been wondering what all the numbers on the cards are for. The numbers are symbols in a classification system. The call number, by which you request the book, tells the librarian in which section of the library, on which shelf, and in which specific place on the shelf the book can be found.

Systems of Classification

The two widely used systems of classification are the Dewey Decimal system and the Library of Congress system. The Dewey Decimal system is the one you will probably use most often. It was developed at Amherst College in 1873 and catalogues all knowledge under *ten divisions.* Each division is assigned a group of numbers.

Dewey Decimal System

Numbers	*Main Divisions*	*Subdivisions*
000–099	General Works	Almanacs, encyclopedias, bibliographies, magazines, newspapers. Materials that cannot be narrowed to a single subject.
100–199	Philosophy	Logic, history of philosophy, systems of philosophy, ethics, and psychology.
200–299	Religion	Sacred writings (the Bible), mythology, history of religions, all religions and theologies.
300–399	Sociology (Social Sciences)	Group dynamics, law, government, education, economics.
400–499	Philology (Study of Linguistics)	Dictionaries dealing with words (not of biographies), grammars and technical studies of all languages.
500–599	Science (Subject and Theoretical)	Astronomy, biology, botany, chemistry, mathematics, physics, etc.
600–699	Applied Science (Useful Arts)	Agriculture, all types of engineering, business, home economics, medicine, nursing, etc.

700–799	Fine Arts. (Professional and Recreative)	Architecture, painting, music, performing arts, sports, etc.
800–899	Literatu e	All types of literature—drama, essays, novels, poetry, etc.—in all languages of all countries.
900–999	History	All history, biography, geography, travel, etc.

If you go to the section of the library labeled Applied Science, 600–699, you will see immediately that the section is divided into subdivisions. For example, 600–610 has general books and collections dealing with applied science. Medicine is classified under 610. Books on engineering begin with 620 and are broken down further by smaller decimals. A glance at the history shelves will reveal that 900–999 classifies general works of history; 910 is geography; and so on by decimal subdivision. English is subdivided into literature of nations and then further catalogued. For example, English literature is 820; English poetry 821; English drama 822; and so on to 829.99. English poetry is further subdivided; 821.1 is early English poetry; and so on to 821.9. Each subdivision designates a specific period. A little observation will make it easy for you to find the exact spot in a particular section of the library where your subject is located.

The Library of Congress system of classification designates the main divisions of knowledge by letters instead of numbers. Subdivisions are made by adding a second letter and whole numbers. We will not give a detailed explanation of this system beyond the classification of knowledge by letter.

Library of Congress System

Letter	*Main Divisions*
A	General Works
B	Philosophy and Religion
C	History—Auxiliary Sciences
D	History—Topography (except American)
E–F	American History—Topography
G	Geography—Anthropology
H	Social Sciences
J	Political Sciences
K	Law
L	Education
M	Music
N	Fine Arts
P	Language–Literature (nonfiction)
Q	Sciences
R	Medicine
S	Agriculture
T	Technology
U	Military Science
V	Naval Science
Z	Bibliography and Library Science
P–Z	Literature (fiction)

Fiction and Biography

Fiction and biography are usually arranged in a section set aside for each, and the cataloguing is usually simplified. Books of fiction are arranged alphabetically by the author's last name. Two or more books by the same author are shelved alphabetically by title. Some libraries use the classification symbol *F* or *Fic* plus the first letter of the author's last name.

Biography is usually classified by the letter *B* or the number *92*. However, some libraries classify individual biographies under *921* and collective biographies under *920*. The *B* and *92* classifications also carry the first letter of the last name of the person written about.

Thus, a biography of Abraham Lincoln is designated B or 92. Biographies are arranged on the shelf alpha-
L L
betically by the last name of the person written about. If there is more than one biography written about the same person, they are arranged alphabetically by author name. Collective biographies are arranged alphabetically according to the author or compiler's name.

Here is a card for collective biography. Some of the information is explained below:

1
920 Rome–Biography
P Plutarch
Plutarch's Lives. The translation
called Dryden's. Corrected from Greek
and revised by A. H. Clough–
2 5 v. Boston, Little, Brown and Co. 1872
3 L.C. DE7. P5 1872 4 8–14601

1 Call number
2 Five volumes
3 Library of Congress Catalogue number
4 Copyright number

With this information fresh in your mind, visit your school or public library. Discover the ease with which you can find your way from one section to another, and remember how to do it so you will not have to roam. Wandering from section to section and from shelf to shelf wastes your time and probably annoys people who are trying to concentrate on their work.

Reference books

In speaking of dictionaries we called the reference

shelf or section of the library an invaluable storehouse of concentrated information. Larger libraries have a whole reference room; the quality of any library is judged by its reference material. Learning how to use reference books is an essential element in improving your grades. Reference books may provide the information you need for a better theme, examination answer, or class report, for they may offer more information than your textbook can include.

Reference books provide a springboard for finding detailed information. You can start in the reference section with only a name or the most meager idea of a topic and find material for an exhaustive study.

Perhaps the first book to catch your eye in the reference section is Webster's Unabridged Dictionary or Funk and Wagnall's New Standard Unabridged Dictionary. Both are so large that they rest on a rack built especially for them. In our study of words we dealt sufficiently with abridged dictionaries; no further explanation is needed. However, a brief explanation of the difference between abridged and unabridged dictionaries is appropriate. Abridged dictionaries include the most important and most used words in the language. The massive unabridged volumes contain practically all the words in the language. Information about each word, especially its origin and history, is sometimes given in more detail than in the abridged dictionary. Both biographical and geographical information is included in the unabridged dictionary. Abbreviations, tables of weights and measurements, meanings of commonly used foreign phrases, and other introductory and glossary information is included. Accessory material is located in either the front or back, depending on the dictionary; Webster's unabridged also divides each page with a horizontal line. At the bottom of the page, below this line, the archaic (old and seldom used) words and foreign phrases are listed. Because some knowledge of abbreviations is essential to successful use of dictionaries, start your study with the section that lists abbreviations.

The word *encyclopedia* comes from the Greek words *enkyklios*, meaning encircle, and *paideia*, meaning education or wisdom. Thus, the encyclopedia "encircles wisdom." Encyclopedias contain authoritative information on an almost unbelievable mass of the world's facts, countries, people, history, laws, definitions, and explanations.

The encyclopedias which you will see most often in school and general public libraries are *World Book* (prepared especially for young people), *Collier's*, *Compton's*, *Funk and Wagnall's*, the *New International*, the *Americana*, and *Britannica*. Libraries also contain encyclopedias (sometimes called cyclopedias) of special subjects and limited fields of knowledge, such as art, science, technology, history, etc. Some encyclopedias limit their scope to particular religions and ethnic groups, such as the *Catholic Encyclopedia*, the *Jewish Encyclopedia*, etc.

Your use of the encyclopedia should start with some knowledge of its purpose, content, arrangement of material, and the abbreviations used throughout. Guide words and letters must also be studied. The encyclopedia will not always give you all the information you want on a topic, although the articles are prepared by experts who often include much detail.

An extensive bibliography is provided either at the end of each article or in a separate volume.

The bibliography (a list of books and articles on the topic) will save you much time when you are working on long themes and research papers. However, many students neglect to check the bibliography provided for a topic in a good encyclopedia. Instead they spend hours skimming volumes and searching the shelves. Some encyclopedias also include a list of *related topics* at the end of important articles. You can use these to broaden your knowledge of the topic without going beyond the encyclopedia.

When you use an encyclopedia you should always check the date of the edition to be sure you are getting the most recent material. There are cases, however, where you would prefer an older edition. For example, a 1920 edition would probably contain more details about a Model T Ford automobile than a 1970 edition. As information on a topic expands, certain earlier facts have to be omitted in favor of more recent ones. If you are writing a paper on a character from ancient times, an older edition might give a more detailed account. However, this is not always true, because archeology and interpretation can throw new light on old topics.

Publishers spend millions of dollars trying to keep their encyclopedias up to date. Frequent revision is one method they use. Many also publish an annual supplement, called a yearbook, which contains new material on many topics. Consequently, it is important to check yearbooks for new information on the topic you are studying.

Although encyclopedias generally contain from

twelve to thirty volumes, a group of smaller reference books is also available. Besides yearbooks, these include one- or two-volume encyclopedias. The one-volume *Columbia Encyclopedia* has information on an amazing number of topics. Inexpensive yearbooks such as the *World Almanac* and the *Information Please Almanac* contain up-to-date statistics, some valuable facts pertaining to government agencies and personnel, and much miscellaneous information on new topics, scientific developments, etc. Both national and state governments issue yearbooks of various kinds. These can be a great help if you are preparing a paper on contemporary developments. You should also be acquainted with the *Statesman's Yearbook* which contains information and statistics on governments and developments in all the countries of the world. In addition, atlases answer questions about geographical locations, size, population statistics, development of natural resources, etc.

Most reference sections also contain numerous biographical dictionaries. Some are devoted solely to musicians, writers, scientists, statesmen, etc. Others, such as *Who's Who in America* and the *Dictionary of American Biography*, sketch the lives of famous persons in all professions. *Current Biography*, published several times a year in magazine form and put in book form each year, gives facts on people who are currently prominent.

Special atlases, books of quotations, gazetteers, handbooks, and books of facts are some of the many additional volumes available to help you find what you need quickly from the reference department. Browse in the reference section of your school or public library, and get acquainted with what is available and its general location. This will save you time later.

Magazines, records, and films

In addition to the contemporary material contained in yearbooks, many interesting and valuable articles are too recent to be found in books. The *Reader's Guide to Periodical Literature* (periodical refers to magazines) and the *New York Times Index* are two chief sources for locating such articles. The *Reader's Guide*, published twice a month, lists alphabetically by author, subject, and title the significant articles, poems, short stories, etc., contained in more than 100 magazines. Be sure to study carefully the *Key to Abbreviations* which follows the list of magazines indexed at the front of the *Guide*. For newspaper articles or editorials the *New York Times Index*, issued monthly, gives the most complete listing and is available in most libraries.

Many school and public libraries have very complete audiovisual departments. They include recordings of famous speeches; color slides of paintings; architectural illustrations; and geographical, historical, and biographical material.

Recent developments in the field of microcard, microfilm, and microprint have reduced large amounts of print to unbelievably small dimensions. By using the microfilm reading machine you can read leading magazines and newspapers to find a specific article.

Perhaps the best way to end this chapter is to simply state that tests given to both high school and college students reveal that those who make the highest grades are those who know how to use the library and *use* it. It is most conducive to study and provides the greatest storehouse of material from which to learn. So learn to use it to improve your grades, widen your horizons, and enlarge your life.

Summary of practices for better library use

1. Form the library habit. The library is a place for quiet study and exciting discovery.
2. Learn the meaning of "call number" and the use of *author*, *title*, and *subject* catalogue cards.
3. Know the Dewey Decimal system and where the several divisions are located in your school or public library.
4. Know how your library arranges fiction and biography. Arrangements vary from one library to another.
5. Study the reference section to learn generally what is available, its location, and how it may be used.
6. Learn to make a working bibliography as you find material on the topic you are studying. Check several model bibliographies at the end of an article in one or two encyclopedias. Make your bibliography on index cards so you can rearrange it at will. Know the difference between a working and an exhaustive bibliography. An exhaustive or complete bibliography lists everything ever written on the topic. Choose a limited topic, for example, a significant yet not too well-known historical character, and prepare a complete bibliography through a methodical investigation.

CHAPTER 13

Written Work: The Product and Its Package

The nature of the product

Of the several skills you develop in educating yourself—listening, reading, speaking, thinking, and writing—the one which gives your teachers the greatest opportunity to measure your ability and achievements is your writing. It is also the skill which you use without much help from the teacher, for you do most of your written work in class to answer exam questions or out of class when you do themes and research papers.

Certain classroom activities tend to make skills other than writing cooperative efforts between teacher and student. The teacher designs lectures and tests to help you improve your span and depth of listening. Emphasis on the nature of various reading assignments and help in underlining and finding the important facts are usually a part of classroom activity. The teacher frames class questions and discussions to help you develop your capacity to think. If you have difficulty in putting your recitation in order, the teacher can fill in a word and direct your statements into positive channels.

Except for the drills provided in your English classes in the fundamentals—spelling, handwriting, punctuation and capitalization, and structure and pattern—your ability and skill in writing are almost always judged as a finished product. Your writing affects the way all your teachers judge your work, because it is in writing that you offer them what you have learned. Not only is your written work the measure of what you have learned, but it reveals more of your character and your willingness to pursue excellence or accept mediocrity than any other work you do. It is the most important product that you have to sell. You sell it for a grade. As with any other product, quality writing brings a quality price.

The pricing does not begin with the term paper or the big test or theme. Your saleable written product begins with your daily paper, whether it is two sentences, a list of ten words, or five problems in mathematics. It includes not only English papers, as many students mistakenly think, but laboratory reports, all test papers, daily papers, weekly themes, book reviews, term papers, and theses of from 10,000 to 20,000 words.

The *primary purpose* of all written work is either to impart information or develop thought. The *primary requirement* of all written work is that it be presented in an interesting, mechanically correct, and attractive manner. Of course, the quality of a group of problems or a word list is measured only by the degree of correctness and attractiveness; attractiveness means neatness and arrangement. A list of ten words, strung across the page, unnumbered, and illegibly written, means something quite different to the teacher than does a neat and legible list numbered down the page in a straight column. Five problems arranged with symmetry and neatness, each distinctly numbered and each answer marked for easy identification, may bring a better price than the indifferent, sloppy paper, even though both may have the correct answers.

How to judge quality

Even when written work takes the form of a single sentence to answer a question, or a simple paragraph, the primary requirements are still demanded of the writer. One of the best methods of producing quality writing is to approach it with questions and judge it with questions after it is written.

Ask yourself the following questions about the next one- or two-sentence answers you write. These are only starters; add questions of your own. Make them progressively demanding until you feel that you have acquired the ability to sense and produce quality answers and to detect and avoid worthless quantity: Can I start my answer by restating the question and thereby make it easy for the reader to mark my paper? Did I carefully avoid using a pronoun to replace the subject of the question? Does this answer contain the fewest number of words possible to make a quality answer? Is this a generalization that does not answer the question, but is a dishonest attempt to get by, which the teacher will detect immediately? These four questions can change the nature of the answers you write for tests. Copy each on a 3″ x 5″ index card and keep them on your desk until you have memorized them. Ask your teacher if you can keep them before you as you take quizzes and tests.

Perhaps you have had the experience of writing a paragraph and then remembering something you wish you had included. Although it was not too important, it was significant enough to have added to the unity and the completeness of your thought. Asking yourself questions before you write can save you much regret and rewriting. Since a paragraph requires definite pattern and structure as well as content, the questions for it become doubly important. Use the following as starters but add your own: (1) Do I have a complete mental blueprint of what this paragraph is to contain? (2) What topic sentence do I want to convey the topic clearly to my reader? (3) What paragraph pattern will best develop the topic? (4) Will my arrangement of ideas lead naturally from main to supporting ideas? Will my choice of words make my meaning clear? (6) Will this paragraph contain only the material necessary to picture the thought or answer completely? (7) Will it be judged as distinctive quality writing or muddled generalization whose only measure is quantity? (8) Will my concluding statement (summary sentence) convince my reader of my ability to control, condense, and keep meaningful structure throughout?

It might surprise and even annoy you that a simple paragraph demands such planning. However, you should realize that you will probably be marked on hundreds of single-paragraph test answers before you finish your education. You should also remember that all of your themes, long or short, will be judged by the quality of both the sentences and the paragraphs.

This is not to imply that all students are supposed to instantly become talented writers who possess unusual creative ability. Certain obligations are basic to both the gifted and the ungifted: (1) For each written assignment all students are obligated to make the necessary study and inquiry to have a working knowledge of the subject about which they are writing. (2) All students are obligated to present the information in a fluent and effective vocabulary, with coherent and unified sentence and paragraph structure, and with the greatest degree of mechanical perfection possible. (3) Most important of all is the moral obligation to never try to pass off thoughtless, trite, boring, and sloppy written work in order to get by. Print these three basic obligations on cards and keep them on your desk. Read them before you start your written assignments.

All effective written composition presupposes having something to say. Some students feel that to be seen on record is sufficient. Being seen on record merely means filling up space with writing. Space-fillers are frequently the same people who have developed a very affected, decorative handwriting which looks attractive at a distance but is almost impossible to read. Space-fillers are also easily identified by their crude way of repeating generalities, forcing the teacher to read worthless, cut-rate, and meaningless rubbish. The students who accept the basic obligations of written work have thought clearly before they begin to write. They write clearly and meaningfully. They write with such interest that their interest cannot be hidden from the teacher who reads their papers.

If your written work is not clearly understandable, and in the best form of which you are capable, you are either lazy or affected; your teacher will detect it in the first paper you write. If you write on a subject about which you have no sound knowledge, you are dishonest. If you know your subject but do not bother to express your thoughts in the best possible form, you are indifferent and irresponsible. Thus, your written work reveals your whole character. The mark you receive on written work is in many ways a measurement of you as a person.

The nature of the package

Nothing is more rewarding for a teacher than to receive a written paper of such neatness and quality that he or she wishes that it did not end. It is equally true that nothing can cause the teacher so much frustration, such a feeling of ineffective teaching, and such a waste of time as a paper which shows no concern for either form or content.

The trite and the ordinary, the mediocre and the humdrum, and the boring and the unorganized reveal a total indifference to clarity, form, style, and quality. Neglect of grammar, spelling, punctuation, vocabulary, and legibility stamps the writer as one whose chief aim is to get by and whose highest standard is accepted incompetence. From this the teacher can easily judge that the writer lacks any element of appreciation for excellence or even an honest desire to improve.

"But," you reply, "I can't write more legibly." Many students expect the teacher to accept this as a valid reason for lack of neatness and order. Is the teacher supposed to go on trying to decipher an impossible mess, to give proper consideration to illegible content, and to show sympathy and pity? The answer is no. It is the responsibility of the student to write in such a way that his or her work is easily read and understood. The teacher should not accept anything less than this.

Excellence has become somewhat old-fashioned from lack of use. Since you hear "minimum requirement" and "permissible" so often to describe what is acceptable, let us pause to examine this beautiful word "excellence." Make it a part of your vocabulary, and more important, a part of your philosophy of life.

"What is excellent is permanent," wrote Emerson. "But how does this relate to something as simple as the way I write a daily quiz paper?" you ask. Each paper you write confronts you with a choice: you can deal poorly with yourself and produce the minimum or permissible, or you can deal wisely with yourself and produce excellence. If you accept your responsibility for gathering the required information, you will find that excellence is also a part of your presentation.

Has a teacher ever held up one of your papers to the class and remarked on its order, neatness, and the ease with which it can be graded? This is generally referred to as the format of the paper. Here are some considerations which can give the format of your written work the quality of excellence.

Do you follow regulations? At the beginning of a course teachers often lay down certain requirements to be followed during the year: name of student in a particular place on the paper, paper folded or not folded, title in the middle of the first line, quiz questions copied on paper, a line skipped between answers, all answers written in complete sentences, all numbers of questions written to the left of the red margin on the paper, a line omitted between French or Latin sentences to allow for corrections, answers to problems in mathematics underlined and designated *Ans.* for easy recognition. These are only a few of the many elements that help your product approach excellence.

Does your work reveal a sense of pride in presentation that cannot be hidden, regardless of whether or not all your answers are correct and all your thinking clear? If the assignment is a 600-word essay, do you crudely jot down the number of words at the end of each page until you reach the great climax of 608? This is an insult to your reader. Is your paper as neat as you can possibly make it, or is it in pencil when ink was required or in your illegible scrawl which you mistakenly believe others can read because you can decipher it? What about the student who, writing on the laws of Hammurabi, misspells Hammurabi in the title of the paper and then alternates between correct and incorrect spelling throughout the paper? What about the person who brings his or her paper a day late or even an hour late? What about the American history student who, assigned a 3000-word theme, turns in a disorganized 1500 words. When asked "Why?" by his teacher he replies, "I guess I wasn't interested enough." What was lacking?—a sense of pride—without which there can be no excellence.

If you accept the minimum as a standard, you will

get a minimum mark. If you require excellence of yourself, you will get an excellent mark. The same reflections will be mirrored throughout your life. You might be lucky and make an exciting sale or bring in a big account, but if your sense of pride does not demand excellence of you it will show in the way you write the report. If you are not promoted, the answer will be within you. You will not have to ask your employer, "Why?"

Writing regular themes

We can define regular themes, as they concern us here, as written compositions which require more than a paragraph or two. They are distinguished from research or term themes, which require the gathering of material. All themes fall into one of two general classes: compositions of ideas or compositions of images.

The composition of ideas relates information and expounds thought. It includes expository and argumentative writing, such as essays, long examination answers, etc. Themes assigned in history and science courses fall into this class.

The composition of images is generally associated with an English assignment, although in advanced English courses themes of criticism and explanation would be considered compositions of ideas. The composition of images deals with narrative and descriptive writing and may take the form of story, description, poetry, or drama.

Many students misunderstand the basic purpose of theme assignments and as a result miss the most important contribution that such assignments make to their education. The primary purpose is not to get a grade, although your aim should always be to get the best grade possible. The first objective of theme assignments is to help the student gain proficiency in writing. This can only be achieved if the criticisms given by the teacher are carefully noted and a sincere effort is made not to repeat the same errors again and again.

If you can remember your last theme grade but do not know the specific weaknesses which brought about the grade, you are among those who miss the purpose of theme assignments. When a theme is returned to you, keep it in your notebook. When your next theme is assigned, check your weaknesses from the last one before you start to write. A list of types of mistakes and shortcomings and the number that occur on successive themes offers graphic incentive for improvement.

By studying the mistakes you make frequently on two or three themes, you can make yourself an improvement chart. It might appear as follows, although its categories would be tailored to your specific needs:

Certainly, there are few among us who do not enjoy evidence of self-improvement. The improvement chart, which lists your particular shortcomings, can be used to encourage and record your improvement. If you can pinpoint your particular faults, it is better to include them specifically rather than to put them under a general entry. For example, if you make apostrophe and semicolon mistakes more often than others, make individual entries for these under punctuation. Your teachers can probably give you valuable help in preparing your chart.

Improvement Chart for Written Work

Type of Mistakes	Number of Times Occurring					
	1st wk.	2nd wk.	3rd wk.	4th wk.	5th wk.	6th wk.
Spelling	13	10	9	7	4	0
Punctuation						
Points off for lack of neatness	10	5	0	0	0	0
Sentence faults						
Poor paragraph construction						
Topic Sentence						
Development						
Arrangement						
Summary Sentence						
Vocabulary						
Word choice						
Lack of clarity						
Affectation						
Mark Received						

Overall Criticism
Teacher's Comments

First Week

Second Week
Third Week
Fourth Week
Fifth Week
Sixth Week

The Four Steps in Theme Writing

There are four important steps in good theme writing: (1) Choosing the subject or, if assigned by the teacher, deciding upon the point of view. (2) Making studying, and revising the outline. (3) Writing the first copy and making outline revisions if necessary. (4) Writing the final copy.

The subject you choose to write on can influence the grade you get in many ways. Students often make the mistake of choosing one of these four dangerous types of topics: (1) One that is too big—*Country Life in Frost's Poetry* rather than *Country Roads in Frost's Poetry.* (2) A topic outgrown after third grade—*Window Box Plants of City People* rather than *Smog and the Death of Trees.* (3) A topic that is too personal and in poor taste—*My Great Ambition* rather than *The Meaning of Motivation.* (4) A topic that is too controversial and about which you have hearsay opinion rather than factual information—*Why We Should Not Salute the Flag in School* rather than *The Meaning of Patriotism.*

The troubles that arise from choosing a topic that is too big are immediately evident. Nothing worthwhile can be said in 600 or 1000 words on a topic that requires a volume for intelligent coverage. The big topic for a short theme usually ends in generalizations that reflect the writer's lack of information and force the teacher to reread stale and tired facts known by everyone.

Childish and personal topics are generally chosen to avoid any real thinking. Many students have the mistaken idea that 600 words of drivel, which they themselves could scarcely read without embarrassment, on *What I Did* or *What I Think* or *My New Boat*, will satisfy the word requirements and perhaps get them a passing grade. However, a personal experience that can be used for illustration or example must be well thought out and inconspicuously presented.

Controversial topics quickly lose all objectivity and become subject to personal feelings. Other people do not necessarily share your feelings and prejudices. Although the teacher grading your paper would not consciously give you a lower grade for ideas with which he or she was not in agreement, you should remember that human nature is never solely divorced from a judgment.

If the topic is assigned, you have no problems; if not, there are intelligent approaches to selecting a topic. One excellent approach is to use the index of a subject which interests you. Suppose you enjoy reading about Dr. Albert Einstein as a person. By checking the index of a biography of Dr. Einstein or some of his writings, you might come upon these topics: *personal life, family, ideas on teaching, close friends.* If you choose the topic *Thoughts on Teaching*, further reference to Dr. Einstein's writings would give you the basic information. If the topic appeared too broad, you might further narrow it to *Dr. Einstein's Thoughts on Teaching Loyalty*, or to some other narrow topic The index, however, is always a good place to start.

In selecting a topic for an image composition, choose from the world immediately before you. You will write a better paper and get a higher grade for a description of a gnarled and ancient sycamore tree outside your window than for a description of a storm at sea which you have not experienced.

The second step toward a good theme is an outline. If it is necessary to outline (blueprint orally) a simple paragraph, common sense says that a composition of any length will not fall into order without an outline. Make your outline on 3″ x 5″ index cards; record the main topics first. After you have arranged the main topics in the order which will produce the best emphasis, coherence, and unity, outline the supporting topics. The nature of the theme will dictate the order of the outline—chronological, numerical, alphabetical, place, or some other logical order which you have devised to fit the topic.

Do not be afraid to spend some time on the outline. You will save time later in the writing, and your product will be more orderly and complete. Many professional writers spend as much time outlining as they spend in actual writing. You can train yourself to outline orally as you go to and from school or while you are at some physical exercise. This will save you much time. One writer of academic books outlines each chapter while chopping wood.

Even though you might change the outline somewhat after you start to write, outlining one or two themes will convince you of its many advantages. It prevents mistakes in the selection and arrangement of material and ensures a sensible proportion of main and contributing ideas. One of the greatest advantages to outlining is that it leads to the discovery of new ideas, new ways to illustrate a point, and a sense of unity which is totally new to many young writers.

A careful examination of the completed outline is always helpful. Questions are a good method of testing whether or not the outline does what you expect of it: (1) Will the outline move the theme directly forward and hold the interest of the reader? (2) Is the outline sufficiently organized and clear enough for the reader to see it beneath the content? (3) Is the outline free of contradictions and repetitions? (4) Does the outline unite main topics in such a way that the message of the whole theme can be stated in a sentence or two, or in not more than a brief paragraph?

After examining the outline you are ready to write the first draft of the composition. Three practices will prove most helpful in writing the first draft: (1) Leave every other line for changes and corrections. (2) Do not write carelessly even though it is a first draft. (3) Write rapidly and without interruption.

Try to write the first draft as nearly like you wish the final product as possible. Completing each step correctly will make each succeeding one less difficult. Although your major concern with the first draft is to get your ideas in order, do not neglect the mechanics of writing. Careless mistakes have habit-forming effects, and they are likely to show up in the final copy. Some students write a first draft so sloppily that it is totally worthless. These people usually write a first, a second, and a third copy. This is a waste of time which helps develop bad writing habits.

Many students mistakenly believe that writing slowly results in a more thorough job. This is not true. Rapid writing gives a spontaneity that will add life to your composition. Rapidity will also make your writing flow forward smoothly; slow writing will move only by jerks. Rapid writing may also dictate changes in your outline which will improve your theme. Do not be afraid to make such changes; blind adherence to the outline can cause stiff and lifeless spots in your composition. Rapid writing makes revising for the final draft little more than correcting errors in mechanics. The slow writer who has struggled over words, confused sentence constructions, and fragmentized ideas by changes finds revision a major job, equivalent to rewriting the whole theme.

The fourth and final step in good composition writing is the production of the final copy. If possible, let time elapse between the writing of the working draft and the final copy. If you use this period to generally think over and around the topic, you will probably think of ideas to clear up difficult spots, choose words more carefully, and find it easier to detect mechanical mistakes made in the first draft.

When you write the final draft concern yourself with the format and general appearance of the paper. Question the use of modifiers. Unless they make a positive contribution, remove them. Ask yourself what your reaction would be if you were the teacher reading and grading the paper. If you can answer this question sincerely, your grade will probably reflect your sincerity, and your teacher will appreciate you as a student who has a "sense of pride in his work" and is willing to expend the energy necessary to put it into effect.

Summary of suggestions for improving written work

1. Written work reveals ability, desire, and character. It is the most important product that you have to offer in exchange for a grade.

2. The primary requirement of all written work is that it be presented in an interesting, mechanically correct, and attractive manner.
3. Judge the quality of your written composition by questioning its parts, content, and presentation.
4. Observe closely the three basic obligations of all students toward written work: (1) Have a working knowledge of the subject. (2) Present the material in the best possible form and structure. (3) Never pass off inferior work in order to get by.
5. Excellence is the only real quality of written work that is permanent. Excellence in packaging the product (putting written work in an attractive, correct, and neat form) comes from a "sense of pride" in one's work.
6. Adopt practices that will reveal your weaknesses and encourage your improvement. Beginning with the four steps in good composition writing, plot your own methods for adding quality and completeness.

CHAPTER 14

Written Work: Research Themes, Book Reports, and Style

The research theme

If students approach the term paper or research theme as a difficult and time-consuming burden, they usually turn out a boring and padded piece of work which boldly betrays their lack of interest. If they consider the theme a challenge and a chance for discovery and creative work, they produce a well-written essay which reflects wide reading and a good grasp of the material, and which is intellectually stimulating to the teacher who reads it.

Originality in the term paper is always of great value; however, your grade is probably derived more from the paper's scope. This refers to the extent of your reading on the subject before you start to write. Originality, like all other forms of inventiveness, is not the gift of all; however, all students can read widely and fulfill the basic obligation of having a good working knowledge of the subject. Only by first studying extensively does the writer arrive at the point where the imaginative consideration of the ideas of others may create new ideas. Usually a new idea is born by combining ideas from other sources. Students who delude themselves by thinking that they can write a successful paper without extensive background reading will be rudely disillusioned by a poor grade.

The padded bibliography is another trap which entangles many who desire to escape the work of acquiring a wide scope of knowledge on the subject about which they are writing. The research paper should indicate that the writer has read several works on the subject and that he has a knowledge of the leading authorities and their particular points of view and contributions to the topic. The research paper most deserving of merit from the standpoint of content is the one which reflects the most contemporary thinking and writing on a particular topic.

All the practices for writing a good composition, especially the outline, are required for writing a research theme. We have seen these in the last chapter; therefore, let us direct ourselves to the best methods of gathering source material.

Some writers use strange and very amusing methods of collecting material. Some gather and store bits of material and ideas the way a squirrel stores nuts. It is said that for thirty years Carl Sandburg gathered stories about Abraham Lincoln and stored them in cigar boxes bearing various subject labels. When Sandburg began his monumental and touchingly beautiful six-volume biography of Lincoln, his cache of cigar-box stories yielded their treasure. Although you will develop your own methods of gathering material, the suggestions offered here provide an orderly and time-saving method for the beginner.

When you gather material for your paper, take notes on 3″ x 5″ index cards. Make a bibliography card for each source. This will save you time when you prepare footnotes and the bibliography after you have written your paper. The bibliography card should contain the following information:

1. Author's full name.
2. Full title of book and edition.
3. Place of publication, publisher, and date of publication or date of edition used.
4. For footnote identification, note volume and page of material used.

Bibliography Card

Audubon, John J.
Birds of America
(Memorial Edition)
New York, Macmillan Co. 1946.
(pages 163–171)

In footnotes the information appears as follows: Audubon, John J., *Birds of America* (memorial edition). New York, Macmillan Co. 1946. (Pages 163–171). In the bibliography all information is listed in the same way; however, the page references are omitted.

The notes you took on material from Audubon would be written on one side only of 3″ x 5″ cards and arranged behind the bibliography card. If you gathered material from five books, the bibliography cards would be numbered one to five and arranged accordingly. An index card for the front of the file is helpful.

Index Card

1. Audubon (Birds of America)
2. Hausman (American Birds)
3. Kieran (Footnotes on Nature)
4. Murray (Wild Wings)
5. Pough (Eastern Land Birds)

Use a single card for each main topic designated by a Roman numeral. When your notes are finished, make a general arrangement; the major outline can later be made from this arrangement. Notes should be brief. Make sure to copy quotations correctly. If the quotations are long, it sometimes saves you time to note only the source and to copy the material directly into the final draft of your paper. This practice is recommended only for material taken from reference books which will be available in the library when you need them.

Bibliography cards should also be made when you gather notes from magazines and newspapers. Pay careful attention to volume, number, and date.

Magazine Bibliography Card

Devoe, Allan, "Our Feathered Friends," Nature Magazine, Vol. 21, No. 10, October, 1951. Pages 21–39.

Newspaper Bibliography Card

The New York Times
"Migrating Birds Hit Empire
State Building"
October 2, 1954. Section 2,
page 4, column 3.

All information from magazine and newspaper cards is usually included in both footnotes and bibliography. The bibliography at the end of your research theme is listed alphabetically by author. Where the author is not given, as in encyclopedias and newspapers, use the first important word of the title. You might find it more convenient to divide your bibliography into sections for books, magazines, and newspapers, in that order. Entries under each are listed alphabetically. Further classification of a bibliography may be for *primary* and *secondary* sources. A theme on an author would list the author's writings as *primary sources*; what others had written about him would be listed as *secondary sources.*

In reading, and in writing your own paper, you will need to know the nature, use, and especially abbreviations of footnotes. Footnotes are more convenient for the reader if they are placed at the bottom of the page to which they refer. However, they are sometimes placed at the end of a section or chapter, or even at the end of a book. For the student's theme, the foot of the page is the best location.

The source of every quotation or summarized passage must be individually acknowledged by the writer; this is the chief use of footnotes. They also serve other purposes, such as defining special terms, giving interesting illustrative material that might not fit naturally into the body of the writing, giving cross references, showing different opinions and points of view, and expressing the writer's indebtedness for an idea. Footnotes are best numbered consecutively by the page when they are arranged at the bottom of the page to which they refer. Some writers use asterisks or other symbols, but these become cumbersome when they are doubled or tripled to indicate two or three footnotes at the bottom of the same page.

In both gathering material and writing your research paper, a knowledge of reference abbreviations is an absolute necessity. Three of the most frequently noted are *ibid* (Latin, meaning in the same place), *opere citato* (Latin, meaning in the works cited), and *loco citato* (Latin, meaning in the place cited). For example, assume that you have three footnotes from Audubon's *Birds of America* on a single page. You would note the first in detail:

[1]Audubon, John J., *Birds of America*, (New York: Macmillan Co., 1946), page 14.

If no other source came between them, the second and third footnotes would be written as follows:

[2]*Ibid.*, page 64.

[3]*Ibid.*, page 73.

If a reference to another source came between them, *op. cit.* (opere citato) or *loc. cit.* (loco citato) could be used as follows:

Audubon, *op. cit.*, page 84.

Audubon, *loc. cit.* (without page number).

The following abbreviations are also used in footnotes and bibliographies:

anon.–anonymous
c. or ca.–circa (about)
cf.–compare or confer
ch., chaps.–chapter, chapters
col., cols.–column, columns
e.g.–exempli gratia (for example)
et seq.–et sequens (and following)
f., ff.–following page, following pages
fac.–facsimile
fig., figs.–figure, figures
I, II–line, lines
id, idem.–in the same place
i.e.–id est (that is)
ms., mss.–manuscript, manuscripts
n.–note
n.b.–nota bene (note well)
n.d.–no date
no., nos.–number, numbers
n.p–no publisher
n.s.–new series
p., pp.–page, pages
pseud.–pseudonym
sec., secs.–section, sections
sic.–thus
[sic.]–error recopied from original
v.–verse
viz.–namely
vol., vols.–volume, volumes

Footnotes, like a sound bibliography, make your paper more scholarly and interesting. Although it is better to use too many than too few, they can be overdone. Use them to reflect your honesty in recognizing the important sources from which you have gathered information and to add interest to your theme. Observe one or two of your textbooks or several scholarly books in your school library for models of effective footnotes and bibliographies.

Book reports

Another kind of written composition that requires all the good practices of thought, outlining, mechanical correctness, and neatness, plus the ability to deal with a special type of material, is the *book report.* A book report shows how well you have read and understood books you are assigned to read.

A book report is primarily a description or account of the contents of a book, or a synopsis of its story. Like all other related reading and writing activities, a book report is also an exercise in thinking. You relate the content of the book to your own experience; then you put certain thoughts about the content into a form which will give the reader the picture you wish to convey.

There are no special rules or formats for writing book reports. Your teacher will probably give you a format to follow. This will include where to put the title, author, date of publication, and what to use in character study, thread of story, etc.

If the book report is short, it is best to relate the story by using the reporter's four *w*'s—*who, where, when,* and *why.* Even the brief report should contain a statement of the format. Why you liked or disliked the book should not be stated editorially as a blank positive or negative statement. The last element in the brief report concerns the main character or characters. The subtlety by which you deal with the characters should reveal your feeling about the book. The impression you create should be sufficiently graphic to create an atmosphere of personal relationship—you were introduced to these characters, or character; you spoke with them; you saw them in action. From this your reader will be able to judge how much you liked or disliked the book. Short book reports usually contain between 100 and 200 words.

The long book report, which contains between 400 and 500 words, also deals with format, time, place, action, and characters; however, it goes beyond these elements. In the long report, you can also consider the four elements of any piece of writing: (1) the sense, (2) the mood, (3) the attitude, and (4) the style. Keep these elements in mind as you read. Make notes or page references to indicate places where each is effectively revealed, and include these references in your report. The sense of a book is reflected in the action, facts, and statements. Are they possible or are they ridiculous distortions of history, nature, and human relations? Mood is the element which makes you feel affection or resentment toward the book. The mood of the characters and the feelings produced by the words will either please or displease you. This will be reflected in the report you write.

Next to mood, the attitude of the author toward both his material and his reader will influence you the most. You will convert this honesty, fairness, and respect (or dishonesty, unfairness, and disrespect) to questions: Does the author merely want to tell a story? Is he convinced of his own beliefs? Is he laughing up his sleeve as he leads the reader? You will try to answer these questions in your book report. It is probably best to restrict your observations of style to a brief statement on the author's clarity, mechanical correctness, and skill in word selection.

The book report you write has two obligations: (1) to describe the book, and (2) to communicate something of its quality or lack of quality. It fails if it leaves the reader wondering what the book is like as a whole. It can also fail if you set yourself up as a final judge. You can communicate your reaction to a book by what is called "impressionistic criticism."

Avoid the trite and the general superlative. Many a book report becomes ridiculous and meaningless because of padded nonsense. Here are some worthless statements taken from book reports. Be sure to avoid them: "---------------- is one of the greatest writers who ever lived and is ever likely to live." If time has already stamped his work as "classic," you need not repeat time's judgment. "I liked *Lord Jim* because it is one of the most exciting sea stories ever written." But you have not read all the sea stories ever written. You cannot even say, "I think it is one of Joseph Conrad's greatest stories," unless you have read all of Conrad's stories. You can quote an authority on Conrad, but in a book report, which is a very personal kind of composition, even this is of doubtful value. "---------------- is one of the greatest geniuses who has ever written historical novels in any language." If the author is such a genius, your teacher is aware of it. He or she probably assigned you the book because the author is recognized as a genius.

Another quick way to ruin your grade on a book

report is to render premature and baseless judgments of condemnation. You are assigned books in order to develop your taste and appreciation of them. Books cannot be appreciated until a background of knowledge has been acquired to establish a standard of measurement. You are certainly not in a position to dislike a book before you have read it (an opinion often expressed orally by students). You will not be prepared to like or dislike some books you read until you have read others like them, and have acquired a body of knowledge upon which to frame comparisons and base judgments.

Opinions have to be earned. Some of the greatest misunderstandings and shortcomings in life stem from the utterly false axiom that we are all "entitled to our opinions." Your opinion of any book is entirely your affair, once you have read it and are acquainted with enough other books of its type to judge. In writing a book report remember that to dislike intelligently is the approach of the educated person; to project baseless opinion is an identifying stamp of ignorance.

The quality of the book you read (when you are allowed to choose the book) will probably be reflected in the quality of the mark you receive on your book report. If you choose to read cheap, sensational trash, you will probably receive a cheap mark. Since time is so important in the process of education, it seems foolish to waste one's time reading anything less than the best.

The great books display their characters in courageous roles, and lift us up to admire the best that human experience has to offer. Try adventuring first among the classics. Who can resist a book that begins:

"Tom!"

No answer.

"Tom!"

No answer.

"What's gone with that boy, I wonder?

"You Tom!"

No answer.

Thus begins Mark Twain's *The Adventures of Tom Sawyer.*

Who could doubt what lies between the first and last sentence of Stephen Crane's *The Red Badge of Courage*:

"The cold passed reluctantly from the earth, and the retiring fogs revealed an army stretched out on the hills, resting." Two hundred pages later the book ends: "His feet made funnel-shaped tracks in the heavy sand."

What more could have been packed into the opening of Dicken's *A Tale of Two Cities*:

"It was the best of times, it was the worst of times, it was the age of wisdom, it was the age of foolishness, it was the epoch of belief, it was the epoch of incredulity, it was the season of Light, it was the season of Darkness, it was the spring of hope, it was the winter of despair. . . ."

Was there ever a more subtle and effective climax

than the sacrifice of Sydney Carton at the end of the same book:

"It is a far, far better thing that I do, than I have ever done; it is a far, far better rest that I go to than I have ever known."

Do not accept the small until you have given close scrutiny to the great. To adventure with the great is to be lifted up, to walk among the small is to be pulled down.

And what do you think of Dr. Samuel Johnson's statement, "Was there ever yet anything written by mere man that was wished longer by its readers, excepting *Don Quixote, Robinson Crusoe* and *The Pilgrim's Progress*?"

A paperback book by James O'Donnell Bennett (Premier Books, Fawcett Publications, Greenwich, Conn., 1960) entitled *Twenty-Five Best Sellers of the Ages* will open a treasure chest of great books to you. Of Daniel Defoe's *Robinson Crusoe* Bennett writes: "It is an epic of competent man, refusing to go mad, refusing to lose the power of speech; ever patient, ingenious, hoping on and on, not for rescue merely, but for the best as God shall order it, be it rescue or endless waiting, and at the last finding his own soul." Before you write your next book report on a book which you are allowed to choose, you might like to look over *Twenty-Five Best Sellers of the Ages*. If it is not in the library, it may be well worth purchasing.

Developing style

There are a host of witnesses to attest to the fact that it is only through the reading of great writing that a feeling for style and an individual writing style emerge. Lincoln became a great master of poetic prose because he saturated his mind with the poetic prose of the Old Testament. The historian who wishes to write lucid and living history does not start writing; he starts by reading Herodotus, Thucydides, Polybius, Plutarch, Cicero, and Livy. But individual style does not come from imitating; it comes from absorbing, from which in time comes feeling to direct the individual.

Style in writing is not something mysterious and secret that is rationed by the gods to those upon whom they look with favor. All who are willing to practice to produce the best are capable of adding quality, dignity, distinction, clarity, and appeal to what they write. Students who desire to improve their style of writing should consider five things: (1) economy of words, (2) simplicity of structure, (3) pattern of sequence, (4) movement toward climax, and (5) colorings of variety. Each, as you are already aware, is an element of good composition. It is the polish or the roughness, the simplicity or the weakness, which you give to each element that determines your own individual style of writing. It is not enough to put down facts or thoughts as you would make a grocery list or tabulate the sales you have made. Writers who elicit response and stir their readers to admiration add something of themselves. When this is evident, it is recognized by the reader as style. The element of success that your own pleasing style will add to your school writing and grades will become a necessity later in life. Your own style of writing will be your primary tool with which to impress others.

Style grows, to a large degree, out of what you wish

to do with a topic. It is never affectation for the sake of style itself. Style begins with well-directed questions about your topic. What is the nature of the topic? What impression do I wish to convey about it? Do I wish to entertain, inform, teach, lead or drive, appease or argue? Do I wish to reach a universal or local audience, young or old, my subordinates or superiors? Your purpose and the way you handle your subject will relay to the reader the warmth and feeling or the cold indifference of your style. Style is in a real sense the part of your heart that shows in your writing.

Summary of practices for better research themes

1. Strive for originality, but depend on your scope of reading and your grasp of material to determine the quality of your theme.
2. Take notes on 3″ x 5″ index cards, and save time by preparing bibliography cards while you are gathering material.
3. Make footnotes and a sound bibliography reflect the scholarship and authority of your paper.

Practices to Improve Book Reports

1. For short book reports use the four *w*'s—*who, where, when,* and *why* to relate the story.
2. In all book reports show your appreciation or lack of it through your study of the characters or the nature of the book. Avoid editorializing to praise or condemn.
3. Observe closely the two obligations that the book report has to the reader: (1) to describe the book, and (2) to communicate something of its quality or lack of it.

4. Avoid the meaningless superlative and the baseless generalization. There is no "best book ever written" and there is no "greatest literary genius who ever lived."
4 If you are allowed to choose the book you read, select a book of quality. Reading trash is a waste of time, and a report on a cheap book is likely to get the writer a cheap grade.

Summary of the Meaning of Style

1 Only by reading great writing can you develop a feeling for style.
2 Style in writing is not affectation, novelty, artificial coloring, or fashion. It is simplicity and sincerity based upon concern for the reader.
3. Style in writing is that quality which brightens the obscure, makes instruction agreeable, gives depth to the simple, adds distinctiveness to the ordinary, and brings harmony out of discord.
4. Style is only achieved by those who believe in what they write. The heart must know first what words can produce on the page.

CHAPTER 15

Tests and Examinations: The Big Score

The nature of tests to come

Although ideally it should be love of learning, achievement, and self-improvement that prompts all learning, the average student is probably motivated by a more tangible, immediate, and pressuring reason—the requirement for taking and passing tests and examinations. Few high school students are not concerned with the aptitude and achievement tests which they must take to get into college.

Students not planning to attend college will take placement, adaptability, and promotion tests if they are to succeed in whatever field they enter. Promotion in the armed services does not depend on physical prowess and length of service, but rather on the ability to study and pass promotional tests. If you understand the importance of tests and examinations, the best methods of preparation, the common sense required for both a physical and a mental approach to them, how to read instructions and questions correctly, and how to answer them the way the test or teacher expects you to answer, you have acquired the meaning and feeling for tests. This is one of the most valuable psychological attributes that can come from your whole educational experience.

Because some knowledge of the nature of these aptitude and achievement tests may give you added incentive for preparing for tests and examinations in your present school subjects, let us consider a few pertinent facts. The scholastic aptitude tests required by many colleges are used by the colleges to help predict whether or not you are likely to succeed in college. The tests are divided into two categories: (1) verbal, which tests your ability to deal with reading subjects; and (2) mathematical, which indicates your skill in dealing with numbers. Since it has been proved that success in learning depends more and more upon the ability to read with understanding, comprehension plays a large part in the verbal test. The mathematics test attempts to measure your ability to apply given concepts to new situations, that is, your ability to reason. The best preparation for aptitude tests is a background of vocabulary interest, wide reading, and practice in clear thinking.

College entrance achievement tests, which are given on specific subject material, lend themselves to a certain amount of preparation. Sample achievement tests are available in many subjects; you should take them. If possible you should take achievement tests in your best subjects. Many colleges require achievement tests in English and Mathematics, plus one other. Many also require a writing sample in the form of an essay.

If you have mastered the art of dealing with essay questions on your school subjects, and can handle the mechanics and diction of good composition, the writing sample should not prove difficult.

Attitude: The first step

Dr. Francis P. Robinson in his book, *Effective Study*, poses this question: "Did you ever thank a teacher for giving an examination?" At first glance you are not likely to find much in your thinking that would help generate an affirmative answer. The teacher does spend much time preparing the test questions; after you have taken the examination, the teacher spends many hours carefully evaluating your paper. Mistakes are marked so that when your paper is returned you can go over them and perhaps write in corrections so you will not make the same mistakes again.

Do you, like many of your fellow students, consider the test or examination as a personal battle which the teacher wages in an attempt to defeat you, or as a contest in which one tries to outwit the other? If this is your attitude toward tests and examinations, you probably do one of two things when the teacher returns your paper to you. One, you throw it away without bothering to do more than glance through it to see where points were taken off; or two, without checking an incomplete answer against the facts as studied, you approach the teacher and demand to know why points were taken off. This is the most negative of approaches. The difference in attitude can be seen in the difference between two questions: "Why did you take off points on this question?" and "What should I have included which I did not?"

Another attitude that you should avoid is that of fear. Fear of taking tests and examinations results in tension and disturbed thinking which produces blind spots (not being able to remember answers that you knew ten minutes before the test) and careless mistakes. This fear also keeps people from venturing into new areas in life. They may visualize the new method, the better tool, or the strong bridge, but they hesitate until someone else realizes their dreams.

Fear prevents success on tests and examinations because fear conditions the mind for failure. Students who are afraid start in a state of confusion and disorder; thus they throw away the advantages they have accumulated by preparation. Students who approach tests and examinations with fear are almost always characterized by the following: (1) Their mark is considerably lower than their daily recitation marks, sometimes as much as twenty points lower. (2) They complain about the teacher—insufficient explanation, lack of detailed review, etc. (3) They find fault with the test material—too long, not the type of questions expected and studied for, didn't understand the wording of questions, read the word *muckrakers* instead of *mugwumps* and missed the whole point. (4) Their preparation consists of a frantic last-ditch effort, loss of sleep almost to the point of total exhaustion, and often loss of important notes or review material just when they were needed most. (5) Fear compels these students to study for the test with another student. Invariably they choose a study companion who has the same attitude of fear and whose knowledge of the subject is only equal to, or perhaps less than, their own.

If you recognize two or more of these characteristics as behavior patterns which you practice at test and examination time, you should change your attitude as quickly as possible. To continue them is to subject yourself to a climate of tension and fear and to condition yourself for defeat.

A third attitude is wholly positive. It is the attitude of challenge, self-confidence, and content-reliability. Students who accept a test as a challenge to show the teacher the extent of their knowledge of the subject and to improve their grades are stimulated. This stimulation produces the energy needed to think clearly and to act with precision over a longer period of concentration than the daily recitation requires. The attitude of challenge is reflected by enterprising rather than burdensome preparation, and self-confidence develops from this adequate preparation. There is no room for tension and fear. Even a questionable answer is approached by a calculated reliability that a worthwhile answer, although perhaps only partially correct, can be worked out. This attitude requires the relationship between student and teacher, and question and answer, always to be one of cooperative production rather than competitive destruction.

To adopt an attitude of challenge and self-confidence toward tests and examinations, you must first understand the real purposes of tests and examinations.

Reasons for tests and examinations

From the student's point of view, the first reason for tests and examinations is motivation. Few of us are sufficiently self-disciplined and motivated to educate ourselves without direction and requirement.

Being tested periodically on accumulated knowledge is a strong motivating force.

A second reason for tests and examinations is that they provide students with an opportunity to show the extent of their learning. Daily recitation does not provide such an opportunity. An examination gives the students a chance to demonstrate their ability to organize and unify large volumes of material. This is not possible in preparing for day-to-day assignments.

A third reason is that students gain insight into what the teacher considers most important. If test questions deal with main topics and essential principles, the student can accurately estimate the nature of future and larger examinations.

A fourth important reason is that students can discover both their shortcomings and the extent of their progress. By carefully studying their errors; the general areas in which they occur; and whether their pattern reflects difficulty in reading questions, taking sufficient notes, or catching important review hints in class; they can take steps toward correcting their weaknesses. They can also measure their progress in effective expression, their ability to organize ideas and record them rapidly, and most significant of all, whether or not their mental growth is keeping up with the demand of the subject.

The fifth reason for tests and examinations is that they constitute one of the most important learning processes. They require students to make decisions regarding appropriation of time, interpretation of facts, discrimination between essential and supporting ideas, and reasonable distribution of each. Indeed, we may call tests and examinations mind-stretchers.

The teacher also benefits from tests and examinations. Through them he or she is able to measure mental growth more accurately than through daily recitations. Tests and examinations show the teacher which students are willing to expend the energy required to maintain high standards on a big job. They also show the teacher which students are the "phonies," those who may bluff their way through small assignments, but really show their lack of preparation and effort at test time. Tests and examinations reveal to the teacher where his or her teaching can be improved. If a large number of students fall down in a particular area of the subject—word problems, vocabulary, explanation, diction—it is probably a signal that more emphasis is needed in this area. In addition, the teacher's point of view on his or her own subject is often broadened by the sound thinking expressed in students' answers.

Now that you understand the reasons for tests and examinations, and how they benefit both student and teacher, you should not groan when a test is announced. Do not approach it as a burdensome chore or with light indifference. Approach it with an honest and determined effort for self-improvement. If you manage this, your mark will manage itself.

Reviewing for tests and examinations

The most successful review is the one which starts with the second assignment at the beginning of the term and continues as a part of daily preparation throughout the course. Such a review should include a well-organized notebook, a basic vocabulary for the course, important class notes, all weekly and monthly test questions, and a well-marked textbook, indicating the material designated important during the course. In addition, a mental blueprint should be woven into the material, uniting the parts of the subject into a unified whole.

This procedure cannot be stressed too strongly; the student who fails to follow it usually faces an impossible task a week or two before the examination. We all know how complex and difficult it is to learn even a small amount of material thoroughly; thus, the person who attempts a whole term's work in a week is playing a silly, losing game. If your continuous review is carried out from week to week, preparing for a weekly quiz or a monthly test should require no more time than a regular daily assignment; an hour test should not demand more than two hours of review. Your test review should deal largely with recitation rather than rereading. Check main topics for recall; where main headings draw a blank, do a limited amount of rereading. This, plus careful attention to important questions and hints given by the teacher, should complete your quiz and test preparation. Therefore, suggestions for review which follow are directed mainly toward the final examination. Several of the practices can be adapted for use in preparing for smaller tests.

Examinations demand primarily the recall of large amounts of information. The objective examination requires only recall; the essay examination demands recall plus organization and amplification. Since effective recall depends upon study distributed over a long period of time, even your immediate review for an examination should be divided into hourly periods of study which start ten days or two weeks before the examination. Review should never be started later than a week before the exam. Five one-hour review periods spread over five days are far more beneficial than ten hours of attempted study the day before the examination.

A ten-hour session or a five-hour ordeal the day before the examination, or an all-night period of mental exhaustion and confusion, cannot be considered review. It can only be described as a short-sighted, superficial, and futile struggle to cram a great deal of information into one's mind. At most, cramming provides a smattering of information for short-term use only. The information slips away quickly, usually even before the examination can be finished. Its chief function is to overlay what you have learned during the term with confusion.

Just when they need order and clear thinking, many students think it necessary to introduce frenzied disorder into their routine and well-being. Crammers invariably brag about it. This is a front against the inadequacy which they already feel. They are also easily identified as they approach the examination room—they are leafing frantically through their books or shuffling their notes in about the same manner that an electric fan would deal with them. If you can organize no better review than the futile cram session, it is better not to review at all. It is better to enter the exam knowing only 60% of the subject than to confuse that 60% by trying to cram the other 40% into your mind during the last few hours before the exam. It is far better to read a good book, go to a movie, get a good night's sleep, and appear at the exam with a fresh clean look.

Pages could be written on the disastrous effects of cramming; the case histories of its ill results and failure would fill volumes. Let us leave its senselessness and learn ways to make a review less a period of self-torture and more a period of profitable study.

Suggestions for successful review

1. Learn to select what is most important to learn. General principles, formulas and experimental conclusions, vocabularies and rules, historical sequences and literary types, and theories and facts are some of the important items in your courses Be sure to differentiate between opinion and fact. Pay particular attention to material that is emphasized by boldface type, questions, or repeated in summary paragraphs.
2. Listen with such precision during the two weeks before the examination that you miss nothing that is said in class. Even though the teacher may be continuing with new material, there are signs to indicate that important items for review are being made available to you. Listen for such statements as: "In October we studied a case not unlike this one. Remember why it was considered so important." "This is the eighth essential principle we have studied this term. They are all important to an understanding of the course." Most teachers refer in one way or another to almost everything you will see on the examination. Listen for it.

   It is also important to keep your eyes open.

Remember the story of the teacher who filled the blackboard with French and English sentences, vocabulary words, rules, etc., a week before examination time. Nothing was said to explain why all this had been written there, and no one asked. When the students saw the examination, the truth was self-evident. The examination had been on the blackboard for a whole week. Two students smiled and began writing perfect papers; they had seen. The others had looked too, but had seen nothing; they each got about their expected grade.

3. Review by using questions to predict questions. When you have found what you consider important, turn it into a question, or ask yourself how it could be made into a question. This requires discipline, for many students choose the easy method of forming only questions which they know they can answer. However, the easy questions are never the only ones asked on examinations. Be honest; accept the hard ones and prepare answers. Good students can predict close to 90% of an examination.

   Do not confuse prediction that results from thorough study with a guessing game. It does not mean simply trying to outguess the teacher, and doing only spot studying. This is usually fatal. You have often heard the victim lament, "I thought he was going to ask ________________, but he didn't, so I had to blank four whole questions."

4. Review by reorganizing your course material. Where possible, reduce the subject matter to easily remembered divisions. In mathematics these divisions may be definitions, word problems, theorems,

formulas, and general concepts. In history they may be biography, chronology, reform movements (radical), reform movements (conservative), domestic wars, foreign wars, economic problems, civic problems, and religious problems. This is one of the most profitable of all review procedures. At first glance it may appear to hinder unity and continuity of the subject. However, it does just the opposite; it binds the parts of the course into a more workable and understandable unit.

5. Review by changing your point of view. If you have dealt with a subject during the term from the point of view of memorization to receive a credit only, change your point of view to that of application for understanding. The first point of view is a deterrent to successful study; the second is one of study's greatest psychological aids. And unless your mind is prepared, there can be no profitable review.

   Change your point of view from that of observer to participant. If you are reviewing history, put yourself into character. Accept a role—not the king, the general, or the hero—through which you can get a comprehensive feeling for the people you are studying. Be a slave, a common soldier, a person in the street. If you are reviewing a foreign language, imagine that in six weeks you will be allowed to use only this language.

   Reviewing by changing your point of view can be an exciting game. Use your imagination and find new approaches to all your subjects.

6. Make question "terminology" and question "reading" a part of your review. Although certain words

appear in question after question, these key words often mean different things to different teachers. You must know what the teacher expects when the question says *explain*, *evaluate*, *state*, *relate*, *illustrate*, *enumerate*, *describe*, *interpret*, *define*, *diagram*, *compare*, *contrast*, *compare and contrast*. Practice reading chapter-end questions to understand exactly what a question asks for. Note the characteristics of questions that pertain to different subjects. Some subjects lend themselves to specifics; questions in other subjects are very general. Question "knowledge" should be an important part of any review.

Taking tests and examinations

Tests and examinations are generally of two kinds: objective and subjective. Objective, or short-answer, tests require you to recognize correct answers among incorrect ones, or true statements set beside false ones. Objective tests also measure your ability to recall details. Objective questions are usually one of the following types: (1) Recall (filling in blanks): Joseph Conrad was born in ________________ and spent his early years ________________. (2) Recognition (multiple choice): Gandhi learned of civil disobedience from (a) Emerson (b) Gladstone (c) Lincoln (d) Marx (e) Thoreau. Ans. (   ). True and False questions are also considered recognition questions: Mockingbirds belong to the mimic family. (T) Mockingbirds belong to the sparrow family. (F) A third type of recognition question is the matching question. For example, write the number of the phrase which fits the character in the space provided:

1. Founder of Hebrew Nation	2	Lincoln
2. The Great Emancipator	1	Moses
3. Apostle of Peace	4	Gladstone
4. Three times Prime Minister	5	Einstein
5. Scientist and Philosopher	3	Woodrow Wilson

Here are some things that you should consider in approaching objective examinations:

1. Pay particular attention to mechanical instructions; that is, instructions which tell you *where* and *how* to answer questions. Wrong position may result in wrong answers; in any case, answering in ways other than that required may cause the teacher difficulty in grading your paper. Some teachers take off points for not following instructions.
2. The questions are usually numerous; sometimes you do not have to answer all of them. Always answer the questions that you know first and come back to any that you wish to spend time on.
3. Read certain types of objective questions (particularly True-False) so that you observe all qualifying words. These words—*usually*, *always*, *most*, *never*, *some*—give insight into when and under what conditions a statement is or is not correct. Modifiers play their most important role in True-False questions.
4. All objective questions require correct reading. Don't let premeditated opinion cause you to read into the question a word that is not there. This results in wrong answers, and after the examination you are heard to say, "But I thought the question was."
5. Do not change answers too quickly as you check your examination before turning it in. Your first

answer is the more reliable unless you are absolutely sure you have made a mistake. If there is any doubt, leave the first answer.

6. Do not think that neatness and order can be ignored on objective examinations. Words and numbers can be written sloppily or neatly. Neatness begins with the first blank you fill and ends with the way you sign your name.

The second kind of test, the subjective, demands more of the student in both recalling and organizing subject matter. These are usually called "essay" tests; they may be short-answer questions (a paragraph) or discussion questions (a lengthy essay which measures the student's entire scope of knowledge on a particular part of the course). The word "subjective" implies that this kind of examination is more personal than the objective test. It provides students with a greater opportunity to show the extent of their preparation. It also provides the teacher with a chance to make more personal judgments in evaluating the paper. For this reason you should think in terms of what judgment you would make of your answers if you were the teacher.

Essay examinations measure your ability to recall what you have learned, organize it intelligently, and express it clearly and with meaningful interpretation, selection, or application, depending upon what is asked for by the question. The first and most important thing to remember about essay examination questions is that there is no such thing as a *general answer*.

You can write successful essay examinations by practicing a few *must* requirements:

1. Read through all the essay questions before you start to write. Essay examinations demand a rather precise allotment of time for each question. On many discussion questions you can write much more than time allows. Therefore, a sketchy outline (oral or written) is almost a necessity in alloting the time needed for each question. If you recognize key words pertaining to the answer at the first reading, write them in the margin as future aids to recall.
2. When you are ready to answer the first question, write the time alloted to it in the margin of your paper. Then read the question to determine exactly what it asks you to do and what instructions are included for doing it. If the question asks for Alexander's spiritual legacy, it is a waste of time to describe the physical legacy (army, devoted generals, etc.) he received from his father. As in objective questions, qualifying words give the question its explicit meaning. Yet some students read words which are not there into questions. The student who reads *muckrakers* instead of *mugwumps* may write a beautiful answer, but he will get no credit; he answered a question that wasn't asked. The qualifying words of a question are really the directions for answering it. A record of careless mistakes on tests and examinations made by students at Kent School over a five-year period showed that carelessness in reading the question was responsible for 64% of all careless mistakes.
3. Read the question a second time to determine the steps you will take in writing a quality answer. Decide what amount of material is needed to pro-

duce a complete answer. Be sure your answer is not so brief that you exclude important details nor so wordy that you make rambling generalizations. This is the time to complete the mental or key-word outline that you began at your initial reading of the examination. Mentally blueprint the arrangement, significance, and accuracy of topics and accompanying details. Visualize an effective opening statement; if possible, restate part of the question. Never start an answer with a pronoun without an antecedent. Two such beginnings, fatal to a good mark but often used, are: "It is when" and "It is because." Always make the subject of the question the subject of your answer. As you read the question for the second time you must constantly watch for anything that will give your answer an element of vagueness.

4. As you write your answer keep in mind the teacher's preference for style of presentation, use of illustration to show understanding, and what the teacher considers a model answer. If the teacher has complimented you on earlier test papers for the way you handled an answer, try to apply this method to as many questions as possible. Ask yourself the question, "What is the teacher's aim in this particular question?" Make your paper easy to mark. Use signal words and numerals to introduce important facts and series. Number questions to the left of the red margin and skip one or two lines between answers. Remember that the neatly written paper has fewer mistakes and is easier for the teacher to mark.

5 Concentrate on one question at a time and use a

mental system of numbering important points in your answer. Students often "overwrite" or "write away from" questions because they jump ahead and are thinking of a question to come. The teacher has not asked questions which require repeating subject matter, so be careful to keep all answers within the limits set by the questions. An excellent method for avoiding generalizations and worthless "padding" is to mentally number important points as you write them down. Illustrations, specific elaboration, important facts, and explanations to clarify your understanding of a definition or event are all necessary parts of a good essay answer. If you number important items mentally as you write, you will see the difference between what has value (and will add to your mark) and what is worthless.

6. Check over the completed examination paper before you turn it in and after it has been graded and returned to you. You should reserve ten minutes of each examination hour for checking after you have completed the writing. Check for mechanical errors and obvious factual mistakes such as wrong words, incorrect conclusions, transposed characters, etc. As with objective tests, do not change anything in an answer unless you are absolutely sure it is wrong. Rely on your first impression.

You can learn much about writing better examinations and using better methods of study by going over the graded paper after it has been returned. By checking against your book you can see what you omitted that the teacher considered important or how you misinterpreted the qualifying word in a question. If you note such errors carefully, you will not repeat them on the next test.

Summary of rules for reviewing for and taking tests and examinations

1. Review by selecting the important subject matter; concentrate on it rather than on the trivial and incidental.
2. Review by listening for hints and helps given by the teacher just prior to the test.
3. Review by predicting questions for the test. Think how questions can be asked on specific subject matter.
4. Review by reorganizing the subject matter into logical divisions. Keep a sense of unity by being aware of relationships among parts.
5. Review by changing your point of view. Let your imagination add interest to the subject.
6. Review by knowing what "question words" mean. Learn what your teacher expects when certain key words are used.
7. When you take the test or examination read all questions and instructions carefully and repeatedly until you understand exactly what the answer and the presentation of the answer require.
8. Know the general implications of key and qualifying words in both objective and essay questions. Do not, under any circumstances, make an exception for what the qualifying word asks for.
9. On objective tests give the precise answer; on essay tests give the complete answer Always remember that quantity without quality will not get a good grade.

10. Observe all rules of neatness, mechanics, and clarity. The attractive paper that is easy to read gets the better grade.
11. Check your paper carefully before you turn it in. Unless you are absolutely sure you have made a mistake, do not change your answers. The first impression, as psychological tests have shown, is more reliable.
12. Improve all future test and examination grades by carefully checking all returned papers. Note your errors and shortcomings so you will not repeat them on the next test.

CHAPTER 16

Motivation: Each Must Find It for Himself

The reach and the grasp

"Ah, but a man's reach should exceed his grasp, Or what's a heaven for?" Thus wrote Robert Browning in his poem, "Andrea del Sarto," in 1855. Although what is within man's reach today has multiplied beyond the vaguest dream of anyone living in Browning's day, it is still a part of natural law that unless man's dreams exceed what he is momentarily capable of grasping, he stops learning. His life becomes mere survival; finally he is pushed off the stage by a better actor who has developed a greater capacity to reach in his dreams. William Golding makes this point in an exciting book entitled *The Inheritors*, in which he describes how slow-witted Neanderthal man was replaced by a person capable of greater vision–Cro-Magnon man.

"But what has this to do with me?" you ask. Beginning with your endowments and the gifts which grow from these endowments, we have encompassed all of the best study methods and practices. They are within both your grasp and your reach to improve your grades. However, if you are really going to succeed, you must extend the demands you make upon these learning processes to drive you from what you are toward what you can become.

This factor, which determines success or failure both in school and in life, is elusive, difficult to isolate from the whole of one's character, and also impossible to define. It is a combination of interest, ambition, inspiration, moral acceptance of life's importance, a sense of values, and faith in oneself. It is sometimes called by one of the several parts ascribed to it, but generally it is given a name which suggests forward movement and the rhythm of a firm quick step—*motivation.*

The power of motivation lies in striving to be the best, not in merely appearing so. Without motivation, people atrophy and civilizations decline. You can ponder forever what makes one person succeed and another fail. But if you were asked why a great civilization declines, you might answer, "A great civilization declines not because geography changes but because people's minds change." People become satisfied and cease to be excited about learning. Civilization declines when people do not want to do and to know; when work becomes drudgery and love of learning is replaced by resentment and impatience; when the aim of learning becomes social status rather than truth and ennoblement.

What do we really know of this moving purpose, motivation, that so profoundly affects people and na tions? First, we should remind ourselves that motivation is that which strives for what is excellent. Perhaps we can find how much of the whole concept of motivation is within us by looking at some of its components.

What can all the study methods in the world do for you if you lack interest? No one can be interested for you; your parents cannot wish it upon you; your teachers cannot force it upon you. Interest is the basic obligation that you must carry into each classroom. Interest often transforms subject matter from something very dead into something active and alive. As Jacques Maritain puts it in his book, *Education at the Crossroads*, "What is learned should never be passively or mechanically received, as dead information which weighs down and dulls the mind. It must rather be transformed by understanding into the very life of the mind, and thus strengthen the latter, as wood thrown into the fire and transformed into flame makes the fire stronger."[1]

Interest gives work a new dimension. Tom Sawyer discovered it when he had his friends whitewash the fence for him. "Work," he said, "consists of whatever a body is obliged to do, and play consists of whatever a body is not obliged to do." Interest gives obligation tne quality and character of privilege. You can use interest to take the feeling of compulsion out of study. Interest will help you do more and better work than is required. The clockwatcher finds the day long and seemingly endless. The interested worker never has all the time he or she wants. Perhaps interest, as a component of motivation, is best summed up by an

[1]Jacques Maritain, *Education at the Crossroads* (New Haven: Yale University Press, 1943).

old axiom that has long hung on the walls of a classroom at Kent School: "If a man does only what is required of him he is a slave, the moment he does more he is a free man."

What of the ingredient of motivation which we call ambition? It is far more than simple willingness to receive. Alexander the Great, at the age of twenty, inherited a well-equipped army led by brilliant and devoted generals. If Alexander had been content only to receive, the army would soon have belonged to the generals. Students who have jobs waiting or places in their fathers' companies often feel that school is a waste of time. They wait to take over; then they quickly lose their places to someone who has learned that ambition is a positive, purposeful, creative force.

Ambition, like the other ingredients of motivation, can be measured by the drop or by the barrel. It is within your power to inventory whatever ambition is within you. Only you can add up your resources, color them by bold strokes with the brush of imagination, and hold them before you as a bright picture of your abilities.

It is easy to make a check list of your ambitions concerning your school work. In addition, much that will pertain to your life's ambitions should be put on your check list while you are still in school: (1) What are my abilities? (2) What will my ambition require of me? (3) What will success mean in the career or job for which I aim? (4) What will defeat mean? (5) Have I put the proper value upon my life and my time? (6) Will my work provide sufficient inspiration and challenge to save me from complacency and stagnation?

We could continue through some explanation of all the components of motivation, but by now you should see what is happening. We have come full circle and are talking about your gifts as described in Chapter 1. Thus, the only way to understand the meaning of motivation is to understand your own gifts and the uses to which they can be put.

Motivation—imperishable

Let us conclude with two true stories to illustrate a fact: if you show concern for both the better self of which you are capable and your gifts through which you can achieve this better self, motivation will take care of itself.

Not all your papers will be returned with honor grades. When you have done your best and still get a low grade, there will be moments of discouragement, doubt, and depression. When this happens, remind yourself of the following story:

The first scene of the story is set in the wilderness of Indiana. A small boy trudges through the winter forest to a one-room school. After six weeks the school closed and the boy suffered the first of many deeply felt disappointments. By the time he was twenty-two, he had wandered as an itinerant worker and was now a partner in a crossroads store at the edge of a frontier village in Illinois. The store failed and he lost every penny he had saved from seven years' hard labor.

The lesson had been expensive, but he felt that he had learned by hard experience. He would not fail again. Two years of struggle provided him with enough funds to enter a second partnership. This time he would succeed. But within two years the second store had failed. The young man's partner drank up the profits. The person to whom the partners sold the store failed to make his payments, and when the entire stock of goods had been sold, disappeared with the receipts. When the former partner died the young man was left with debts which seemed impossible to ever pay off.

Now he asked a friend to help him get a job as a surveyor, and he studied mathematics with the village schoolmaster to prepare himself for the job. After he was appointed to the surveyor's job, he borrowed money to buy instruments and a horse; however, he never had a chance to begin work. Creditors from his mercantile failures seized his possessions and he lost both horse and instruments.

Immediately after this the gods dealt him the cruelest blow of all, convincing him that he had been singled out for pain and failure from birth. His sweetheart, perhaps a deep and enduring love, the like of which he did not experience again, suddenly died. He descended to the depths of despair and gloom, often pondering whether the struggle to live was worth it. Long afterward he wrote, "At this period of my life I never dared to carry a pocketknife, fearing I would destroy myself."

Time passes. The man no longer looks young, although he is not yet forty. After ten years of struggle he has paid off the last of his debts. While he worked to pay them off, he also spent long hours trying to satisfy his insatiable hunger to learn, to be able to put into words what he felt, to understand the feelings of men around him.

Friends began to suggest that this failure might be a success in the most unexpected of places—politics. So they elected him to Congress. He did not succeed; after two short terms he was defeated for reelection. Nine years later his staunch friends determined to nominate him for the U.S. Senate. However, a split developed in the party and he was forced to step aside in favor of a candidate who could win the number of votes for nomination. This too was failure. Two years later, when he did manage to be nominated and run for the Senate, he was soundly defeated. Of this failure he said, "I was down and out of politics at the age of 50." Looking back over thirty years of his life he could not claim a single personal victory.

The motivating forces of gods and men, of fate, of dreams and destiny, are beyond prediction and comprehension. No man knows when he is walking with destiny, and no man was ever less suspecting than this long-time loser. For in the 52nd year of life, in the 32nd year of failure, this man was elected President of the United States. He is usually listed among the half-dozen greatest men who ever lived. His name, of course, is Abraham Lincoln.

Motivation—a seed falling upon good ground

The second story is really a continuation of the first. Abraham Lincoln had one thing in common with Anthony La Manna. Anthony was born on April 14; the day on which Lincoln was shot. The years were different, however; Lincoln was shot in 1865 and Anthony La Manna was born in 1888 in the village of

Valguarnera Caropepe, amid the stone quarries of Monte Erei.

Anthony La Manna, one of eleven children, entered the quarries as a laborer at the age of twelve. Under the scorching Sicilian sun, amid the deafening ringing of hammers and thunderous thuds and rattles of giant slabs of stone crashing into pits, Anthony La Manna dreamed of nothing beyond the sulphur and rock-salt mines near the sea, where the pay was better. But even these mines seemed far away. They were south over the hills and past the valley through which ran the Assinarus River. Tony could wipe the sweat from his brow and scan the jagged horizon, but the hope of better wages from sulphur or rock-salt mines was far away—perhaps too far.

Few ever went from the quarries. The pattern of trudging up the mountain at sunrise and back down at sunset, with an occasional goatherd to offer news from beyond the hills, became for most the center and circumference of a world.

Anthony La Manna, reading the history of his island with his fifth-grade education, and listening to his elders talk, felt that change was against the natural order of things. Sicily, he thought, had really not changed much in the 2315 years since Nicias and the Athenian army had been destroyed on the banks of the Assinarus River in 415 B.C. The Athenians who were defeated in battle were enslaved in the quarries, where they were scorched by the sun and where they died. Anthony La Manna had also seen men die in the quarries.

When Tony La Manna was sixteen, he followed

the valley and the river down to the sea. In the Gulf of Gela a ship was loading goods to carry to America, and Anthony La Manna "hired on."

There were times in America when Anthony would have given much to be back on the road which led homeward from the quarry, where the friendly voice of the goatherd broke the loneliness. But his four years in the quarries had given him much skill with a chisel and a hammer on stone; after a short time of digging ditches in the swamps of New Jersey, he became a stonecutter's apprentice in Washington, D.C.

Sixteen years in America, aged thirty-two, proud of the only diploma he ever dreamed of possessing—a stonecutter's union card—he is chosen to carve the Gettysburg Address on the Lincoln Memorial. Day after day, as he worked high on the scaffold, he studied the countenance on the gigantic statue. The sad, tired man, who had begun life in surroundings as humble as those of Tony La Manna, had become a lawyer, and a President. He had saved his country in its most trying hour and had given voice to the immortal words that a Sicilian immigrant boy was now writing in stone to be "forever enshrined" in the hearts of men.

One day at lunch time, as Tony La Manna sat on the end of the high scaffold looking into the middle section of the great monument, where sat the rail splitter from the wilderness of Illinois, the stone splitter from Monte Erei made a sudden decision—Anthony La Manna could make something more of himself. He would become a lawyer. On a piece of planking he wrote "Anthony LaManna" and under his name "Attorney at Law." At the end of the day he brought the piece of board down from the scaffold His friends laughed—"Another Aba Lincoln maybe Tony, you looka too much at the statue."

It's a long way from a noisy fifth grade class in the little stuccoed school in Caropepe, Sicily, to the National Law Center at George Washington University in Washington, D.C. After ten hours on a scaffold with chisel and hammer, there was night school—"Engulesh, how you say in Engulesh! Noun, verb, what for pronoun, adjudgtive?" And in his canvas bag with chisels, hammer, and salami sandwiches, Tony La Manna carried books. He would hurry through his lunch and begin to read. His friends would laugh, as long before Lincoln's rail-splitting companions had laughed at him, as he sat on a stump with a book in one hand and a slab of salt pork between two chunks of cornbread in the other.

Finally Anthony La Manna was admitted to law school. But World War I came, and he went away to fight for democracy and the right to be free and learn and become something in America. When he came back he earned an LL.B. and an LL.M. in rapid succession.

For nearly forty years he was a successful lawyer in both New York and Washington, and was special counselor to the Veteran's Administration for thirty-two years. When I asked him if I could tell his story to illustrate the meaning of motivation, he thought I should find a better example. When I asked him to describe what he considered motivation, he said, "Impossible, for each man must discover and define it for himself."

So ends the story, the chapter, and this book. What

is motivation and from whence does it come? The answer is as difficult to describe as trying to tell the direction of the wind by hearing it move through far-off hills at night. Unless you find your own answer to what motivation is, you will never know. If you have it, you will know; if you do not have it, those around you will know.

You can escape neither time nor history. Unless you use the gifts you have been given, time will close many doors which open on long corridors of opportunity through which you will never be permitted to walk. As you turn your back on the closed doors to walk in the tracks you have already made, you will find history gazing upon you, holding you accountable for misappropriation.

"Of what?" you demand.

"Of your talents," answers history.

BIOLOGY
EUROPEAN HISTORY
& WORLD CULTURES

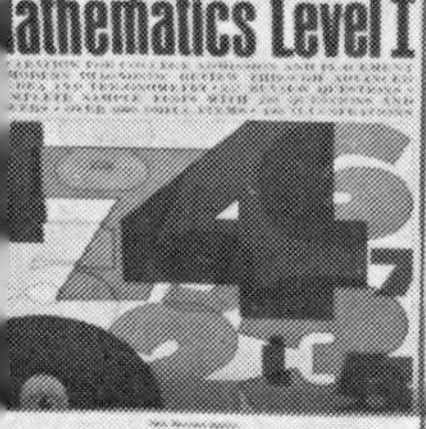

athematics Level I

German

Chemistry

french
Practical Hints Exam Techniques
10 Model Exams with Answers and Explanations Self-Scoring System
Latest Listening-Reading Tests
Idioms Reading Skills Word Study
Mastery of Grammar Over 1500 Practice Questions Verb Charts
Vocabulary Lists

PHYSICS

ENGLISH

How to Prepare for College Entrance Examinations (SAT)

Revised Eighth Edition

Samuel C. Brownstein and Mitchel Weiner 660 pp. $4.95

More than 1.75 million college-bound students have found help with their SAT review. The newly revised Eighth Edition features 6 model examinations that are patterned after the SAT exam now being given. All test questions presented with answers explained to help students learn from their errors. With comprehensive math and verbal reviews. The verbal review offers the basic word list and practice answering questions on analogies, reading comprehension, synonyms and antonyms, and sentence completion. The math review emphasizes the new quantitative comparison question recently added to the SAT. In addition, there is thorough practice and review for the new Test of Standard Written English, also recently added to the SAT. Added bonus section includes model Achievement Tests for the English Composition, Biology, Chemistry, Physics, French, German, Spanish, and Math Level 1.

At your local bookseller or order direct adding 10% postage plus applicable sales tax.

Barron's Educational Series, Inc., 113 Crossways Pk. Dr., Woodbury, N.Y. 11797

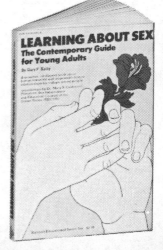

Notes

Notes

Notes